BLACKSTONE GRIDDLE COOKBOOK:

2 Books in 1: 200 Flavorful Recipes for Beginners andAdvanced Pitmasters, learn how to Grill meat with specific instruction.

Mark Franklin

BLACKSTONE GRILL

© Copyright 2021 - All rights reserved.

The content contained within this book may not be reproduced, duplicated or transmitted without direct written permission from the author or the publisher.

Under no circumstances will any blame or legal responsibility be held against the publisher, or author, for any damages, reparation, or monetary loss due to the information contained within this book. Either directly or indirectly.

Legal Notice:

This book is copyright protected. This book is only for personal use. You cannot amend, distribute, sell, use, quote or paraphrase any part, or the content within this book, without the consent of the author or publisher.

Disclaimer Notice:

Please note the information contained within this document is for educational and entertainment purposes only. All effort has been executed to present accurate, up to date, and reliable, complete information. No warranties of any kind are declared or implied. Readers acknowledge that the author is not engaging in the rendering of legal, financial, medical or professional advice. The content within this book has been derived from various sources. Please consult a licensed professional before attempting any techniques outlined in this book.

By reading this document, the reader agrees that under no circumstances is the author responsible for any losses, direct or indirect, which are incurred as a result of the use of information contained within this document, including, but not limited to, errors, omissions, or inaccuracies.

Table Of Contents

© Copyright 2021 - All rights reserved. 2
Disclaimer Notice: 2

GRILL BEEF RECIPES 9
Beef Tenderloin 10
Mustard Beef Short Ribs 11
Sweet & Spicy Beef Brisket 12
Brandy Beef Tenderloin 13
Beef Rump Roast 14
Herbed Prime Rib Roast 15
Spicy Chuck Roast 16

GRILL PORK RECIPES 17
Smoked Avocado Pork Ribs 17
Smoked Honey - Garlic Pork Chops 18
Smoked Pork Burgers 19
Smoked Pork Chops Marinated with Tarragon 20
Smoked Pork Cutlets in Citrus-Herbs Marinade 21
Smoked Pork Cutlets with Caraway and Dill 22
Smoked Pork Loin in Sweet-Beer Marinade 23
Smoked Pork Ribs with Fresh Herbs 24
Smoked Pork Side Ribs with Chives 25
Smoked Spicy Pork Medallions 26
Applewood Smoked Mango Pork Quesadillas 27

GRILL LAMB RECIPES 29
Grilled Lamb Burgers 30
Grilled Lamb Sandwiches 31
Lamb Chops 32
Lamb Ribs Rack 33
Lamb Shank 34

GRILL POULTRY RECIPES 35
Blackstone Chile Lime Chicken 36
Blackstone Grilled Buffalo Chicken 37
Blackstone Sheet Pan Chicken Fajitas 38
Blackstone Asian Miso Chicken wings 39
Yan's Grilled Quarters 40
Cajun Patch Cock Chicken 41

TURKEY, RABBIT AND VEAL 43
Wild Turkey Egg Rolls 44
Trager Smoked Spatchcock Turkey 45
Grilled Filet Mignon 46
Buttery Apple Smoked Turkey 47
Smoked Turkey Legs   grill 48
Smoked Turkey in Beer Brine 49
Hot Smoked Turkey with Jelly Glaze 50

SMOKING   RECIPES 51
Smoked Ribs 51
Smoked Pot Roast 52

- Smoked Brisket 53
- Blackstone Smoked Potatoes 54

FISH AND SEAFOOD RECIPES 55
- Grilled Lobster Tail 56
- Halibut 57
- Grilled Salmon 58
- Barbeque Shrimp 59
- Blackstone Grilled Tuna steaks 60
- Oyster in Shells 61
- Grilled King Crab Legs 62
- Cajun Smoked Catfish 63
- Smoked Scallops 64
- Grilled Tilapia 65
- Blackstone Salmon with Togarashi 66

VEGETARIAN RECIPES 67
- Kale Chips 68
- Sweet Potato Fries 69
- Potato Fries with Chipotle Peppers 70
- Blackstone Grilled Zucchini 71
- Smoked Potato Salad 72
- Baked Parmesan Mushrooms 73
- Roasted Spicy Tomatoes 74

VEGAN RECIPES 75
- Wood Pellet Smoked Mushrooms 76
- Wood Pellet Grilled Zucchini Squash Spears 77

RED MEAT RECIPES 79
- Chipotle Honey Smoked Beef Roast 79
- Lemon Chili Smoked Beef Brisket 100

BAKING RECIPES 102
- Quick Yeast Dinner Rolls 103
- Baked Cornbread with Honey Butter 104
- S'mores Dip with Candied Pecans 105

CHEESE AND BREAD 106
- Blackstone-Grill Flatbread Pizza 106
- Blackstone Smoked Nut Mix 108

APPETIZERS AND SIDES 109
- Atomic Buffalo Turds 109
- Grilled Corn 110
- Thyme - Rosemary Mash Potatoes 111

MORE SIDES 112
- Grilled Mushroom Skewers 112
- Caprese Tomato Salad 114
- Watermelon-Cucumber Salad 115

SNACKS 116
- Corn Salsa 117
- Nut Mix on the Grill 118

DESSERT RECIPE 120

- Grilled Pineapple with Chocolate Sauce 120
- Nectarine and Nutella Sundae 121
- Cinnamon Sugar Donut Holes 122

SAUCES AND RUBS 124
- Heavenly Rabbit Smoke 124
- Uncle Johnny's Rub 125
- Fajita Seasoning 126

NUT AND FRUIT RECIPES 128
- Smoked Bananas Foster Bread Pudding 128

TRADITIONAL RECIPES 130
- Sweet & Spicy Chicken Thighs 130

SAUCES, RUBS, AND MARINATES 132
- Classic Kansas City BBQ Sauce 132

RUBS, INJECTABLES, MARINADES, AND MOPS 134
- Not-Just-For-Pork Rub 134
- Chicken Rub 135

OTHER RECIPES YOU NEVER THOUGHT ABOUT TO GRILL 136
- Summer Treat Corn 136
- Crunchy Potato Wedges 137
- Twice Grilled Potatoes 138
- Mouthwatering Cauliflower 139
- Super-Addicting Mushrooms 140
- Veggie Lover's Burgers 141
- Satisfying Veggie Casserole 142
- North American Pot Pie 143
- Potluck Favorite Baked Beans 144
- Traditional English Mac n' Cheese 145
- Amazing Irish Soda Bread 146
- Native Southern Cornbread 147

CONCLUSION 148

GRILL BEEF RECIPES 2
- BBQ Spiced Flank Steak 3
- Beef Stuffed Bell Peppers 4
- BBQ Meatloaf 5
- Smoked Beef Brisket in Sweet and Spicy Rub 6
- Simple Smoked Beef Brisket with Mocha Sauce 7
- Lemon Ginger Smoked Beef Ribs 8
- Chocolate Smoked Beef Ribs 9

GRILL PORK RECIPES 10
- Simple Wood Pellet Smoked Pork Ribs 10
- Roasted Pork with Balsamic Strawberry Sauce 11
- Wood Pellet Grill Pork Crown Roast 12
- Wet-Rubbed St. Louis Ribs 13
- Cocoa Crusted Pork Tenderloin 14
- Wood Pellet Grilled Bacon 15
- Wood Pellet Grilled Pork Chops 16
- Wood Pellet Blackened Pork Chops 17

- Teriyaki Pineapple Pork Tenderloin Sliders 18
- Wood Pellet Grilled Tenderloin with Fresh HerbSauce 19
- Wood Pellet Grilled Shredded Pork Tacos 20

GRILL LAMB RECIPES 22
- Lamb Shank 23
- Leg of a Lamb 24
- Lamb Breast 25
- Smoked Lamb Shoulder Chops 26

GRILL POULTRY RECIPES 28
- Roasted Tuscan Thighs 29
- Smoked Bone In-Turkey Breast 30
- Teriyaki Smoked Drumstick 31
- Hickory Smoke Patchcock Turkey 32
- Lemon Cornish Chicken Stuffed with Crab 33
- Bacon Cordon Blue 34

TURKEY, RABBIT AND VEAL 36
- Lightly Spiced Smoked Turkey 37
- BBQ Pulled Turkey Sandwiches 38
- Tempting Tarragon Turkey Breasts 39
- Juicy Beer Can Turkey 40
- Buttered Thanksgiving Turkey 41
- Jalapeno Injection Turkey 42
- Turkey Meatballs 43

SMOKING RECIPES 44
- Blackstone Smoked devil Eggs 44
- Cajun Smoked Turkey Recipe 45
- CCRyder's Cider-Smoked Ribs Recipe 46
- Fat Boy's Smoked Baby Backs Recipe 47

FISH AND SEAFOOD RECIPES 48
- Trager Rockfish 49
- Blackstone Grilled Lingcod 50
- Crab Stuffed Lingcod 51
- Blackstone Smoked Shrimp 53
- Grilled Shrimp Kabobs 54
- Sweet Bacon-Wrapped Shrimp 55
- Blackstone Spot Prawn Skewers 56
- Blackstone Bacon-wrapped Scallops 57
- Blackstone Lobster Tail 58
- Roasted Honey Salmon 59
- Blackened Salmon 60
- Grilled Cajun Shrimp 61

VEGETARIAN RECIPES 62
- Blackstone Smoked Mushrooms 63
- Grilled Zucchini Squash Spears 64
- Grilled Asparagus & Honey-Glazed Carrots 65
- Blackstone Grilled Vegetables 66
- Smoked Acorn Squash 67
- Roasted Green Beans with Bacon 68
- Smoked Watermelon 69
- Grilled Corn with Honey Butter 70

- Smoked Mushrooms 71
- Smoked Cherry Tomatoes 72

VEGAN RECIPES 100
- Wood Pellet Cold Smoked Cheese 101
- Wood Pellet Grilled Asparagus and Honey Glazed Carrots 102

RED MEAT RECIPES 104
- Strip Steak Smoked and Seared 104
- Smoked Corned Beef Brisket 105

BAKING RECIPES 106
- Brown Sugared Bacon Cinnamon Rolls 107
- Blackstone Soft Gingerbread Cookie 108
- Sweet Pull-Apart Rolls 109

CHEESE AND BREAD 110
- Blackstone Grill Chicken Flatbread 110
- Grilled Homemade Croutons 111

APPETIZERS AND SIDES 112
- Grilled Broccoli 112
- Smoked Coleslaw 113
- The Best Potato Roast 114

MORE SIDES 116
- Fresh Creamed Corn 116
- Spinach Salad with Avocado and Orange 117
- Raspberry and Blue Cheese Salad 118

SNACKS 120
- Grilled French Dip 121
- Roasted Cashews 122

DESSERT RECIPE 124
- Pellet Grill Chocolate Chip Cookies 124
- Delicious Donuts on a Grill 125
- Smoked Pumpkin Pie 126

SAUCES AND RUBS 128
- Herbed Mixed Salt 128
- Classic BBQ Rub 129
- Garlic and Rosemary Meat Rub 130

NUT AND FRUIT RECIPES 132
- Grilled Pound Cake with Fruit Dressing 132

TRADITIONAL RECIPES 134
- Bacon Wrapped Chicken Breasts 134

SAUCES, RUBS, AND MARINATES 136
- Garlic-Salt Pork Rub 136

RUBS, INJECTABLES, MARINADES, AND MOPS 138
- Dill Seafood Rub 138
- Cajun Rub 139

OTHER RECIPES YOU NEVER THOUGHT ABOUT TO GRILL...............140
- Decadent Chocolate Cheesecake..140
- Pork Tenderloin Sandwiches..142
- Cheesy Ham and Pineapple Sandwich..143
- Garlic Parmesan Grilled Cheese Sandwiches..144
- Grilled Pizza Cheese..145
- Turkey Pesto Panini...146
- Grilled Veggie Panini..147
- Greek Chicken Salad Pita Pockets...148
- Mini Portobello Burgers..149
- Layered Beef & Corn Burger..150
- Prosciutto Pesto Hot Dog...151
- Bacon Jalapeno Wraps..152

CONCLUSION..153

GRILL BEEF RECIPES

Beef Tenderloin

Preparation Time: 10 minutes

Cooking Time: 1 hour 19 minutes

Servings: 12

Ingredients:

- 1 (5-pound) beef tenderloin, trimmed
- Kosher salt, as required
- ¼ cup olive oil
- Freshly ground black pepper, as required

Directions:

1. With kitchen strings, tie the tenderloin at 7-8 places.
2. Season tenderloin with kosher salt generously.
3. With a plastic wrap, cover the tenderloin and keep aside at room temperature for about 1 hour.
4. Preheat the Z Grills Blackstone Grill & Smoker on grill setting to 225-250 degrees F.
5. Now, coat tenderloin with oil evenly and season with black pepper.
6. Arrange tenderloin onto the grill and cook for about 55-65 minutes.
7. Now, place cooking grate directly over hot coals and sear tenderloin for about 2 minutes per side.
8. Remove the tenderloin from the grill and place onto a cutting board for about 10-15 minutes before serving.
9. With a sharp knife, cut the tenderloin into desired-sized slices and serve.

Nutrition: Calories 425 Total Fat 21.5 g Saturated Fat 7.2 g Cholesterol 174 mg Sodium 123 mg Total Carbs 0 g Fiber 0 g Sugar 0 g Protein 54.7 g

Mustard Beef Short Ribs

Preparation Time: 15 minutes
Cooking Time: 3 hours
Servings: 6
Ingredients:

For Mustard Sauce:

- 1 cup prepared yellow mustard
- ¼ cup red wine vinegar
- ¼ cup dill pickle juice
- 2 tablespoons soy sauce
- 2 tablespoons Worcestershire sauce
- 1 teaspoon ground ginger
- 1 teaspoon granulated garlic

For Spice Rub:

- 2 tablespoons salt
- 2 tablespoons freshly ground black pepper
- 1 tablespoon white cane sugar
- 1 tablespoon granulated garlic

For Ribs:

- 6 (14-ounce) (4-5-inch long) beef short ribs

Directions:

1. Preheat the Z Grills Blackstone Grill & Smoker on smoke setting to 230-250 degrees F, using charcoal.
2. For sauce: in a bowl, mix together all ingredients.
3. For rub: in a small bowl, mix together all ingredients.
4. Coat the ribs with sauce generously and then sprinkle with spice rub evenly.
5. Place the ribs onto the grill over indirect heat, bone side down.
6. Cook for about 1-1½ hours.
7. Flip the side and cook for about 45 minutes.
8. Flip the side and cook for about 45 minutes more.
9. Remove the ribs from grill and place onto a cutting board for about 10 minutes before serving.
10. With a sharp knife, cut the ribs into equal sized individual pieces and serve.

Nutrition: Calories 867 Total Fat 37.5 g Saturated Fat 13.7 g Cholesterol 361 mg Sodium 3462mg Total Carbs 7.7 g Fiber 2.1 g Sugar 3.6 g Protein 117.1 g

Sweet & Spicy Beef Brisket

Preparation Time: 10 minutes
Cooking Time: 7 hours
Servings: 10
Ingredients:

- 1 cup paprika
- ¾ cup sugar
- 3 tablespoons garlic salt
- 3 tablespoons onion powder
- 1 tablespoon celery salt
- 1 tablespoon lemon pepper
- 1 tablespoon ground black pepper
- 1 teaspoon cayenne pepper
- 1 teaspoon mustard powder
- ½ teaspoon dried thyme, crushed
- 1 (5-6-pound) beef brisket, trimmed

Directions:

1. In a bowl, place all ingredients except for beef brisket and mix well.
2. Rub the brisket with spice mixture generously.
3. With a plastic wrap, cover the brisket and refrigerate overnight.
4. Preheat the Z Grills Blackstone Grill & Smoker on grill setting to 250 degrees F.
5. Place the brisket onto grill over indirect heat and cook for about 3-3½ hours.
6. Flip and cook for about 3-3½ hours more.
7. Remove the brisket from grill and place onto a cutting board for about 10-15 minutes before slicing.
8. With a sharp knife, cut the brisket in desired sized slices and serve.

Nutrition: Calories 536 Total Fat 15.6 g Saturated Fat 5.6 g Cholesterol 203 mg Sodium 158 mg Total Carbs 24.8 g Fiber 4.5 g Sugar 17.4 g Protein 71.1 g

Brandy Beef Tenderloin

Preparation Time: 15 minutes

Cooking Time: 2 hours 2 minutes

Servings: 6

Ingredients:

For Brandy Butter:

- ½ cup butter
- 1 ounce brandy

For Brandy Sauce:

- 2 ounces brandy
- 8 garlic cloves, minced
- ¼ cup mixed fresh herbs (parsley, rosemary and thyme), chopped
- 2 teaspoons honey
- 2 teaspoons hot English mustard

For Tenderloin:

- 1 (2-pound) center-cut beef tenderloin
- Salt and cracked black peppercorns, as required

Directions:

1. Preheat the Z Grills Blackstone Grill & Smoker on grill setting to 230 degrees F.
2. For brandy butter: in a pan, melt butter over medium-low heat.
3. Stir in brandy and remove from heat.
4. Set aside, covered to keep warm.
5. For brandy sauce: in a bowl, add all ingredients and mix until well combined.
6. Season the tenderloin with salt and black peppercorns generously.
7. Coat tenderloin with brandy sauce evenly.
8. With a baster-injector, inject tenderloin with brandy butter.
9. Place the tenderloin onto the grill and cook for about ½-2 hours, injecting with brandy butter occasionally.
10. Remove the tenderloin from grill and place onto a cutting board for about 10-15 minutes before serving.
11. With a sharp knife, cut the tenderloin into desired-sized slices and serve.

Nutrition: Calories 496 Total Fat 29.3 g Saturated Fat 15 g Cholesterol 180 mg Sodium 240 mg Total Carbs 4.4 g Fiber 0.7 g Sugar 2 g Protein 44.4 g

Beef Rump Roast

Preparation Time: 10 minutes
Cooking Time: 6 hours
Servings: 8
Ingredients:

- 1 teaspoon smoked paprika
- 1 teaspoon cayenne pepper
- 1 teaspoon onion powder
- 1 teaspoon garlic powder
- Salt and ground black pepper, as required
- 3 pounds beef rump roast
- ¼ cup Worcestershire sauce

Directions:

1. Preheat the Z Grills Blackstone Grill & Smoker on smoke setting to 200 degrees F, usingcharcoal.
2. In a bowl, mix together all spices.
3. Coat the rump roast with Worcestershire sauce evenly and then, rub with spice mixture generously.
4. Place the rump roast onto the grill and cook for about 5-6 hours.
5. Remove the roast from the grill and place onto a cutting board for about 10-15 minutes before serving.
6. With a sharp knife, cut the roast into desired-sized slices and serve.

Nutrition: Calories 252 Total Fat 9.1 g Saturated Fat 3 g Cholesterol 113 mg Sodium 200 mg Total Carbs 2.3 g Fiber 0.2 g Sugar 1.8 g Protein 37.8 g

Herbed Prime Rib Roast

Preparation Time: 10 minutes

Cooking Time: 3 hours 50 minutes

Servings: 10

Ingredients:

- 1 (5-pound) prime rib roast
- Salt, as required
- 5 tablespoons olive oil
- 2 teaspoons dried thyme, crushed
- 2 teaspoons dried rosemary, crushed
- 2 teaspoons garlic powder
- 1 teaspoon onion powder
- 1 teaspoon paprika
- ½ teaspoon cayenne pepper
- Ground black pepper, as required

Directions:

1. Season the roast with salt generously.
2. With a plastic wrap, cover the roast and refrigerate for about 24 hours.
3. In a bowl, mix together remaining ingredients and set aside for about 1 hour.
4. Rub the roast with oil mixture from both sides evenly.
5. Arrange the roast in a large baking sheet and refrigerate for about 6-12 hours.
6. Preheat the Z Grills Blackstone Grill & Smoker on smoke setting to 225-230 degrees F, using pecan wood chips.
7. Place the roast onto the grill and cook for about 3-3½ hours.
8. Meanwhile, preheat the oven to 500 degrees F.
9. Remove the roast from grill and place onto a large baking sheet.
10. Place the baking sheet in oven and roast for about 15-20 minutes.
11. Remove the roast from oven and place onto a cutting board for about 10-15 minutes before serving.
12. With a sharp knife, cut the roast into desired-sized slices and serve.

Nutrition: Calories 605 Total Fat 47.6 g Saturated Fat 17.2 g Cholesterol 135 mg Sodium 1285

Spicy Chuck Roast

Preparation Time: 10 minutes
Cooking Time: 4½ hours
Servings: 8
Ingredients:

- 2 tablespoons onion powder
- 2 tablespoons garlic powder
- 1 tablespoon red chili powder
- 1 tablespoon cayenne pepper
- Salt and ground black pepper, as required
- 1 (3 pound) beef chuck roast
- 16 fluid ounces warm beef broth

Directions:

1. Preheat the Z Grills Blackstone Grill & Smoker on grill setting to 250 degrees F.
2. In a bowl, mix together spices, salt and black pepper.
3. Rub the chuck roast with spice mixture evenly.
4. Place the rump roast onto the grill and cook for about 1½ hours per side.
5. Now, arrange chuck roast in a steaming pan with beef broth.
6. With a piece of foil, cover the pan and cook for about 2-3 hours.
7. Remove the chuck roast from grill and place onto a cutting board for about 20 minutes before slicing.
8. With a sharp knife, cut the chuck roast into desired-sized slices and serve.

Nutrition: Calories 645 Total Fat 48 g Saturated Fat 19 g Cholesterol 175 mg Sodium 329 mg Total Carbs 4.2 g Fiber 1 g Sugar 1.4 g Protein 46.4 g

GRILL PORK RECIPES

Smoked Avocado Pork Ribs

Preparation Time: 20 Minutes
Cooking Time: 3 Hours
Servings: 5
Ingredients:

- 2 lbs. of pork spare ribs
- 1 cup of avocado oil
- One teaspoon of garlic powder
- One teaspoon of onion powder
- One teaspoon of sweet pepper flakes
- Salt and pepper, to taste

Directions:

1. In a bowl, combine the avocado oil, garlic salt, garlic powder, onion powder, sweet pepper flakes, and salt and pepper.
2. Place pork chops in a shallow container and pour evenly avocado mixture.
3. Cover and refrigerate for at least 4 hours or overnight.
4. Start pellet grill on, lid open until the fire is established (4-5 minutes).
5. Increase the temperature to 225 and pre-heat for 10 - 15 minutes.
6. Arrange pork chops on the grill rack and smoke for 3 to 4 hours.
7. Transfer pork chops on serving plate, let them rest for 15 minutes, and serve.

Nutrition: Calories: 677 call Carbohydrates: 0.9g Fat: 64g Fiber: 0.14g Protein: 28.2g

Smoked Honey - Garlic Pork Chops

Preparation Time: 15 Minutes
Cooking Time: 60 Minutes
Servings: 4
Ingredients:

- 1/4 cup of lemon juice freshly squeezed
- 1/4 cup honey (preferably a darker honey)
- Three cloves garlic, minced
- Two tablespoons of soy sauce (or tamari sauce)
- Salt and pepper to taste
- 24 ounces center-cut pork chops boneless

Directions:

1. Combine honey, lemon juice, soy sauce, garlic, and salt and pepper in a bowl.
2. Place pork in a container and pour marinade over pork.
3. Cover and marinate in a fridge overnight.
4. Remove pork from marinade and pat dry on kitchen paper towel. (Reserve marinade)
5. Start your pellet on Smoke with the lid open until the fire is established (4 - 5 minutes).
6. Increase temperature to 450 and preheat, lid closed, for 10 - 15 minutes.
7. Arrange the pork chops on the grill racks and smoke for about one hour (depending on the thickness)
8. In the meantime, heat the remaining marinade in a small saucepan over medium heat to simmer.
9. Transfer pork chops on a serving plate, pour with the marinade, and serve hot.

Nutrition: Calories: 301.5 call Carbohydrates: 17g Fat: 6.5g Fiber: 0.2g Protein: 41g

Smoked Pork Burgers

Preparation Time: 15 Minutes
Cooking Time: 1 Hour and 45 Minutes
Servings: 4
Ingredients:

- 2 lb. ground pork
- 1/2 of onion finely chopped
- 2 Tablespoon fresh sage, chopped
- One teaspoon garlic powder
- One teaspoon cayenne pepper
- Salt and pepper to taste

Directions:

1. Start the pellet grill on SMOKE wait until the fire is established.
2. Set the temperature to 225 and warm-up, lid closed, for 10 to 15 minutes.
3. In a bowl, combine ground pork with all remaining ingredients.
4. Use your hands to mix thoroughly—form mixture into eight evenly burgers.
5. Place the hamburgers on the racks.
6. Smoke the burgers for 60 minutes until they reach an internal temperature of 150 to 160.
7. Serve hot.

Nutrition: Calories: 588.7 call Carbohydrates: 1g Fat: 48.2g Fiber: 0.5g Protein: 38.4g

Smoked Pork Chops Marinated with Tarragon

Preparation Time: 20 Minutes
Cooking Time: 3 Hours
Servings: 4
Ingredients:

- 1/2 cup olive oil
- 4 Tablespoon of fresh tarragon chopped
- Two teaspoons fresh thyme, chopped
- Salt and grated black pepper
- Two teaspoon apple cider vinegar
- Four pork chops or fillets

Directions:

1. Whisk the olive oil, tarragon, thyme, salt, pepper, apple cider, and stir well.
2. Place the pork chops in a container and pour it with a tarragon mixture.
3. Refrigerate for 2 hours.
4. Start pellet grill on, lid open, until the discharge is established (4-5 minutes). Increase the temperature to 225 and allow to pre-heat, lid closed, for 10 - 15 minutes.
5. Remove chops from marinade and pat dry on kitchen towel.
6. Arrange pork chops on the grill rack and smoke for 2 to 3 hours.
7. Transfer chops on a serving platter and lets it rest 15 minutes before serving.

Nutrition: Calories: 528.8 Cal Carbohydrates: 0.6g Fat: 35g Fiber: 0.14g Protein: 51g

Smoked Pork Cutlets in Citrus-Herbs Marinade

Preparation Time: 4 Hours

Cooking Time: 1 Hour and 45 Minutes

Servings: 4

Ingredients:

- Four pork cutlets
- One fresh orange juice
- Two large lemons freshly squeezed
- Ten twigs of coriander chopped
- 2 Tablespoon of fresh parsley finely chopped
- Three cloves of garlic minced
- 2 Tablespoon of olive oil
- Salt and ground black pepper

Directions:

1. Place the pork cutlets in a large container along with all remaining ingredients; toss to cover well.
2. Refrigerate at least 4 hours or overnight.
3. When ready, remove the pork cutlets from marinade and pat dry on a kitchen towel.
4. Start pellet grill on, lid open until the fire is established (4-5 minutes). Upsurge the temperature to 250 and allow to pre-heat, lid closed, for 10 - 15 minutes.
5. Place pork cutlets on grill grate and smoke for 1 1/2 hours.
6. Serve hot.

Nutrition: Calories: 260 Cal Carbohydrates: 5g Fat: 12g Fiber: 0.25g Protein: 32.2g

Smoked Pork Cutlets with Caraway and Dill

Preparation Time: 4 Hours

Cooking Time: 1 Hour and 45 Minutes

Servings: 4

Ingredients:

- Four pork cutlets
- Two lemons freshly squeezed
- Two tablespoons fresh parsley finely chopped
- 1 Tablespoon of ground caraway
- 3 Tablespoon of fresh dill finely chopped
- 1/4 cup of olive oil
- Salt and ground black pepper

Directions:

1. Place the pork cutlets in a large resealable bag and all remaining ingredients; shake to combine well.
2. Refrigerate for at least 4 hours.
3. Remove the pork cutlets from marinade and pat dry on a kitchen towel.
4. Start the pellet grill (recommended maple pellet) on SMOKE with the lid open until the fire is established.
5. Set the temperature to 250 and preheat for 10 to 15 minutes.
6. Arrange pork cutlets on the grill rack and smoke for about 1 1/2 hours.
7. Allow cooling at room temperature before serving.

Nutrition: Calories: 308 Cal Carbohydrates: 2.4g Fat: 18.5g Fiber: 0.36g Protein: 32g

Smoked Pork Loin in Sweet-Beer Marinade

Preparation Time: 15 Minutes
Cooking Time: 3 Hours
Servings: 6
Ingredients:

Marinade

- One onion finely diced
- 1/4 cup honey (preferably a darker honey)
- 1 1/2 cups of dark beer
- 4 Tablespoon of mustard
- 1 Tablespoon fresh thyme finely chopped
- Salt and pepper

Pork

- 3 1/2 lbs. of pork loin

Directions:

1. Combine all fixings for the marinade in a bowl.
2. Place the pork along with marinade mixture in a container, and refrigerate overnight.
3. Remove the pork from the marinade and dry on a kitchen towel.
4. Prepare the grill on Smoke with the lid open until the fire is established.
5. Set the temperature to 250F and preheat, lid closed, for 10 to 15 minutes.
6. Place the meat on the grill rack and smoke until the pork's internal temperature is at least 145-150 (medium-rare), 2-1/2 to 3 hours.
7. Remove meat from the smoker and let rest for 15 minutes before slicing.
8. Serve hot or cold.

Nutrition: Calories: 444.6 Cal Carbohydrates: 17g Fat: 12.7g Fiber: 0.8g Protein: 60.5g

Smoked Pork Ribs with Fresh Herbs

Preparation Time: 20 Minutes
Cooking Time: 3 Hours
Servings: 6
Ingredients:

- 1/4 cup olive oil
- 1 Tablespoon garlic minced
- 1 Tablespoon crushed fennel seeds
- One teaspoon of fresh basil leaves finely chopped
- One teaspoon fresh parsley finely chopped
- One teaspoon fresh rosemary finely chopped
- One teaspoon fresh sage finely chopped
- Salt and ground black pepper to taste
- 3 lbs. pork rib roast bone-in

Directions:

1. Combine the olive oil, garlic, fennel seeds, parsley, sage, rosemary, salt, and pepper in a bowl; stir well.
2. Coat each chop on equal sides with the herb mixture.
3. Start the pellet grill (recommended hickory pellet) on SMOKE with the lid open until the fire is established. Set the temperature to 225 and heat up, lid closed, for 10 to 15 minutes.
4. Smoke the ribs for 3 hours.
5. Transfer the ribs to a platter and serve hot.

Nutrition: Calories: 459.2 Cal Carbohydrates: 0.6g Fat: 31.3g Fiber: 0.03g Protein: 41g

Smoked Pork Side Ribs with Chives

Preparation Time: 15 Minutes
Cooking Time: 3 Hours and 20 Minutes
Servings: 6
Ingredients:

- 1/3 cup of olive oil (or garlic-infused olive oil)
- 3 Tablespoon of ketchup
- 3 Tablespoon chives finely chopped
- 3 lbs. of pork side ribs
- Salt and black pepper to taste

Directions:

1. In a bowl, stir together olive oil, finely chopped chives, ketchup, salt, and pepper.
2. Cut pork into individual ribs and generously coat with chives mixture.
3. Flinch the pellet grill on SMOKE with the lid open until the discharge is established.
4. Set the temperature to 250 and preheat for 10 to 15 minutes.
5. Arrange pork chops on the grill rack and smoke for about 3 to 4 hours.
6. Allow resting 15 minutes before serving.

Nutrition: Calories: 689.7 Cal Carbohydrates: 2g Fat: 65g Fiber: 0.1g Protein: 35.2g

Smoked Spicy Pork Medallions

Preparation Time: 15 Minutes
Cooking Time: 1 Hour and 45 Minutes
Servings: 6
Ingredients:

- 2 lb. pork medallions
- 3/4 cup chicken stock
- 1/2 cup tomato sauce (organic)
- 2 Tablespoon of smoked hot paprika (or to taste)
- 2 Tablespoon of fresh basil finely chopped
- 1 Tablespoon oregano
- Salt and pepper to taste

Directions:

1. In a bowl, blend the chicken stock, tomato sauce, paprika, oregano, salt, and pepper.
2. Brush bigheartedly over the outside of the tenderloin.
3. Twitch the pellet grill on Smoke with the lid open until the fire is established (4 to 5 minutes). Set the temperature to 250 and preheat, lid closed, for 10 to 15 minutes.
4. Place the pork on the grill grate and smoke until the pork's internal temperature is at minimum medium-rare (about 145) for 1 1/2 hours.
5. Let meat rest for 15 minutes and serve.

Nutrition: Calories: 364.2 Cal Carbohydrates: 4g Fat: 14.4g Fiber: 2g Protein: 52.4g

Applewood Smoked Mango Pork Quesadillas

Preparation Time: 10 Minutes
Cooking Time: 15 Minutes
Servings: 4
Ingredients:

- One tablespoon olive oil
- 1.7 pounds Smithfield Applewood Smoked Bacon Pork Loin Filet cut into little scaled-down pieces
- One teaspoon chipotle stew powder pretty much to your taste
- One teaspoon smoked paprika
- 4-inch flour tortillas 6-8
- One ready yet firm mango, stripped + diced
- 1 cup cooked rice or quinoa
- 2 cups destroyed sharp cheddar
- Cherry tomato salsa:
- 2 cup cherry tomatoes
- One jalapeno seeded + hacked
- 1/4 cup new basil cleaved
- 1/4 cup fresh cilantro cleaved
- Juice from 1/2 a lime
- Salt to taste

Directions:

1. Warmth a heavy skillet over medium heat and include olive oil, contain the pork, and season with chipotle bean stew pepper and paprika. Cook, regularly mixing until the pork is caramelized, all finished around 8 minutes. Expel from the warmth. Expel the pork to a plate.
2. Utilizing a similar skillet, over medium warmth, include a touch of olive oil. Spot 4 tortillas down on a perfect counter, sprinkle each with destroyed cheddar, at that point equally appropriate the rice, and top with the hacked mango pieces. Presently include the pork, cut into little scaled-down pieces. Sprinkle with somewhat more of the cheddar. Spot the tortilla onto the hot frying pan or skillet and spread with the other tortilla. Cook until the base is firm and brilliant dark-colored. At that point, tenderly flip and cook for another 2-3 minutes until fresh and bright.
3. Present with the tomato salsa and cut avocado.

Nutrition: Calories: 477 Cal Carbohydrates: 4.5g Fat: 14g Fiber: 2.4g Protein: 50g

GRILL LAMB RECIPES

Grilled Lamb Burgers

Preparation Time: 10 minutes
Cooking Time: 15 minutes
Servings: 5
Ingredients:

- 1 1/4 pounds of ground lamb.
- 1 egg.
- 1 teaspoon of dried oregano.
- 1 teaspoon of dry sherry.
- 1 teaspoon of white wine vinegar.
- 4 minced cloves of garlic.
- Red pepper
- 1/2 cup of chopped green onions.
- 1 tablespoon of chopped mint.
- 2 tablespoons of chopped cilantro.
- 2 tablespoons of dry bread crumbs.
- 1/8 teaspoon of salt to taste.
- 1/4 teaspoon of ground black pepper to taste.
- 5 hamburger buns.

Directions:

1. Preheat a Wood Pellet Smoker or Grill to 350-450 degrees F then grease it grates.
2. Using a large mixing bowl, add in all the ingredients on the list aside from the buns then mix properly to combine with clean hands.
3. Make about five patties out of the mixture then set aside.
4. Place the lamb patties on the preheated grill and cook for about seven to nine minutes turning only once until an inserted thermometer reads 160 degrees F.
5. Serve the lamb burgers on the hamburger, add your favorite toppings and enjoy.

Nutrition: Calories: 376 Cal Fat: 18.5 g Carbohydrates: 25.4 g Protein: 25.5 g Fiber: 1.6 g

Grilled Lamb Sandwiches

Preparation Time: 5 minutes
Cooking Time: 50 minutes
Servings: 6
Ingredients:

- 1 (4 pounds) boneless lamb.
- 1 cup of raspberry vinegar.
- 2 tablespoons of olive oil.
- 1 tablespoon of chopped fresh thyme.
- 2 pressed garlic cloves.
- 1/4 teaspoon of salt to taste.
- 1/4 teaspoon of ground pepper.
- Sliced bread.

Directions:

1. Using a large mixing bowl, add in the raspberry vinegar, oil, and thyme then mix properly to combine. Add in the lamb, toss to combine then let it sit in the refrigerator for about eight hours or overnight.
2. Next, discard the marinade the season the lamb with salt and pepper to taste. Preheat a Wood Pellet Smoker and grill t0 400-500 degrees F, add in the seasoned lamb and grill for about thirty to forty minutes until it attains a temperature of 150 degrees F.
3. Once cooked, let the lamb cool for a few minutes, slice as desired then serve on the bread with your favorite topping.

Nutrition: Calories: 407 Cal Fat: 23 g Carbohydrates: 26 g Protein: 72 g Fiber: 2.3 g

Lamb Chops

Preparation Time: 10 minutes
Cooking Time: 12 minutes
Servings: 6
Ingredients:

- 6 (6-ounce) lamb chops
- 3 tablespoons olive oil
- Ground black pepper

Directions:

1. Preheat the pallet grill to 450 degrees F.
2. Coat the lamb chops with oil and then, season with salt and black pepper evenly.
3. Arrange the chops in pallet grill grate and cook for about 4-6 minutes per side.

Nutrition: Calories: 376 Cal Fat: 19.5 g Carbohydrates: 0 g Protein: 47.8 g Fiber: 0 g

Lamb Ribs Rack

Preparation Time: 10 minutes
Cooking Time: 2 hours
Servings: 2
Ingredients:

- 2 tablespoons fresh sage
- 2 tablespoons fresh rosemary
- 2 tablespoons fresh thyme
- 2 peeled garlic cloves
- 1 tablespoon honey
- Black pepper
- ¼ cup olive oil
- 1 (1½-pound) trimmed rack lamb ribs

Directions:

1. Combine all ingredients
2. While motor is running, slowly add oil and pulse till a smooth paste is formed.
3. Coat the rib rack with paste generously and refrigerate for about 2 hours.
4. Preheat the pallet grill to 225 degrees F.
5. Arrange the rib rack in pallet grill and cook for about 2 hours.
6. Remove the rib rack from pallet grill and transfer onto a cutting board for about 10-15 minutes before slicing.
7. With a sharp knife, cut the rib rack into equal sized individual ribs and serve.

Nutrition: Calories: 826 Cal Fat: 44.1 g Carbohydrates: 5.4 g Protein: 96.3 g Fiber: 1 g

Lamb Shank

Preparation Time: 10 minutes
Cooking Time: 4 hours
Servings: 6
Ingredients:

- 8-ounce red wine
- 2-ounce whiskey
- 2 tablespoons minced fresh rosemary
- 1 tablespoon minced garlic
- Black pepper
- 6 (1¼-pound) lamb shanks

Directions:

1. In a bowl, add all ingredients except lamb shank and mix till well combined.
2. In a large resealable bag, add marinade and lamb shank.
3. Seal the bag and shake to coat completely.
4. Refrigerate for about 24 hours.
5. Preheat the pallet grill to 225 degrees F.
6. Arrange the leg of lamb in pallet grill and cook for about 4 hours.

Nutrition: Calories: 1507 Cal Fat: 62 g Carbohydrates: 68.7 g Protein:163.3 g Fiber: 6 g

GRILL POULTRY RECIPES

Blackstone Chile Lime Chicken

Preparation Time: 2 Minutes
Cooking Time: 15 Minutes
Servings: 1

Ingredients

- 1 chicken breast
- 1 tbsp oil
- 1 tbsp spice ology Chile Lime Seasoning

Directions:

1. Preheat your Blackstone to 4000F.
2. Brush the chicken breast with oil then sprinkle the chile-lime seasoning and salt.
3. Place the chicken breast on the grill and cook for 7 minutes on each side or until the internal temperature reaches 1650F.
4. Serve when hot and enjoy.

Nutrition: Calories 131, Total fat 5g, Saturated fat 1g, Total carbs 4g, Net carbs 3g Protein 19g, Sugars 1g, Fiber 1g, Sodium 235mg

Blackstone Grilled Buffalo Chicken

Preparation Time: 5 Minutes
Cooking Time: 10 Minutes
Servings: 6

Ingredients

- 5 chicken breasts, boneless and skinless
- 2 tbsp homemade BBQ rub
- 1 cup homemade Cholula Buffalo sauce

Directions:

1. Preheat the Blackstone to 4000F.
2. Slice the chicken breast lengthwise into strips. Season the slices with BBQ rub.
3. Place the chicken slices on the grill and paint both sides with buffalo sauce.
4. Cook for 4 minutes with the lid closed. Flip the breasts, paint again with sauce, and cook until the internal temperature reaches 1650F.
5. Remove the chicken from the Blackstone and serve when warm.

Nutrition: Calories 176, Total fat 4g, Saturated fat 1g, Total carbs 1g, Net carbs 1g Protein 32g, Sugars 1g, Fiber 0g, Sodium 631mg

Blackstone Sheet Pan Chicken Fajitas

Preparation Time: 10 Minutes
Cooking Time: 10 Minutes
Servings: 10
Ingredients

- 2 lb. chicken breast
- 1 onion, sliced
- 1 red bell pepper, seeded and sliced
- 1 orange-red bell pepper, seeded and sliced
- 1 tbsp salt
- 1/2 tbsp onion powder
- 1/2 tbsp granulated garlic
- 2 tbsp Spice ologist Chile Margarita Seasoning
- 2 tbsp oil

Directions:

1. Preheat the Blackstone to 4500F and line a baking sheet with parchment paper.
2. In a mixing bowl, combine seasonings and oil then toss with the peppers and chicken.
3. Place the baking sheet in the Blackstone and let heat for 10 minutes with the lid closed.
4. Open the lid and place the veggies and the chicken in a single layer. Close the lid and cook for 10 minutes or until the chicken is no longer pink.
5. Serve with warm tortillas and top with your favorite toppings.

Nutrition: Calories 211, Total fat 6g, Saturated fat 1g, Total carbs 5g, Net carbs 4g Protein 29g, Sugars 4g, Fiber 1g, Sodium 360mg

Blackstone Asian Miso Chicken wings

Preparation Time: 15 Minutes
Cooking Time: 25 Minutes
Servings: 6

Ingredients

- 2 lb. chicken wings
- 3/4 cup soy
- 1/2 cup pineapple juice
- 1 tbsp sriracha
- 1/8 cup miso
- 1/8 cup gochujang
- 1/2 cup water
- 1/2 cup oil
- Togarashi

Directions:

1. Preheat the Blackstone to 3750F
2. Combine all the ingredients except togarashi in a zip lock bag. Toss until the chicken wings are well coated. Refrigerate for 12 hours
3. Pace the wings on the grill grates and close the lid. Cook for 25 minutes or until the internal temperature reaches 1650F
4. Remove the wings from the Blackstone and sprinkle Togarashi.
5. Serve when hot and enjoy.

Nutrition: Calories 703, Total fat 56g, Saturated fat 14g, Total carbs 24g, Net carbs 23g Protein 27g, Sugars 6g, Fiber 1g, Sodium 1156mg

Yan's Grilled Quarters

Preparation Time: 20 minutes (additional 2-4 hours marinade)
Cooking Time: 1 to 1.5 hours
Servings: 4

Ingredients:

- 4 fresh or thawed frozen chicken quarters
- 4-6 glasses of extra virgin olive oil
- 4 tablespoons of Yang's original dry lab

Directions:

1. Configure a wood pellet smoker grill for indirect cooking and use the pellets to preheat to 325 ° F.
2. Place chicken on grill and cook at 325 ° F for 1 hour.
3. After one hour, raise the pit temperature to 400 ° F to finish the chicken and crisp the skin.
4. When the inside temperature of the thickest part of the thighs and feet reaches 180 ° F and the juice becomes clear, pull the crispy chicken out of the grill.
5. Let the crispy grilled chicken rest under a loose foil tent for 15 minutes before eating.

Nutrition: Calories 956, Total fat 47g, Saturated fat 13g, Total carbs 1g, Net carbs 1g Protein 124g, Sugars 0g, Fiber 0g, Sodium 1750mg

Cajun Patch Cock Chicken

Preparation Time: 30 minutes (additional 3 hours marinade)
Cooking Time: 2.5 hours
Servings: 4

Ingredients:

- 4-5 pounds of fresh or thawed frozen chicken
- 4-6 glasses of extra virgin olive oil
- Cajun Spice Lab 4 tablespoons or Lucile Bloody Mary Mix Cajun Hot Dry Herb Mix Seasoning

Directions:

1. Use hickory, pecan pellets, or blend to configure a wood pellet smoker grill for indirect cooking and preheat to 225 ° F.
2. If the unit has a temperature meat probe input, such as a MAK Grills 2 Star, insert the probe into the thickest part of the breast.
3. Make chicken for 1.5 hours.
4. After one and a half hours at 225 ° F, raise the pit temperature to 375 ° F and roast until the inside temperature of the thickest part of the chest reaches 170 ° F and the thighs are at least 180 ° F.
6. Place the chicken under a loose foil tent for 15 minutes before carving.

Nutrition: Calories 956, Total fat 47g, Saturated fat 13g, Total carbs 1g, Net carbs 1g Protein 124g, Sugars 0g, Fiber 0g, Sodium 1750mg

TURKEY, RABBIT AND VEAL

Wild Turkey Egg Rolls

Preparation Time: 10 minutes
Cooking Time: 55 minutes
Servings: 1
Ingredients:

- Corn - ½ cup
- Leftover wild turkey meat - 2 cups
- Black beans - ½ cup
- Taco seasoning - 3 tablespoon
- Water ½ cup
- Rotel chilies and tomatoes - 1 can
- Egg roll wrappers- 12
- Cloves of minced garlic- 4
- 1 chopped Poblano pepper or 2 jalapeno peppers
- Chopped white onion - ½ cup

Directions:

1. Add some olive oil to a fairly large skillet. Heat it over medium heat on a stove.
2. Add peppers and onions. Sauté the mixture for 2-3 minutes until it turns soft.
3. Add some garlic and sauté for another 30 seconds. Add the Rotel chilies and beans to the mixture. Keeping mixing the content gently. Reduce the heat and then simmer.
4. After about 4-5 minutes, pour in the taco seasoning and 1/3 cup of water over the meat. Mix everything and coat the meat well. If you feel that it is a bit dry, you can add 2 tablespoons of water. Keep cooking until everything is heated all the way through.
5. Remove the content from the heat and box it to store in a refrigerator. Before you stuff the mixture into the egg wrappers, it should be completely cool to avoid breaking the rolls.
6. Place a spoonful of the cooked mixture in each wrapper and then wrap it securely and tightly. Do the same with all the wrappers.
7. Preheat the Blackstone grill and brush it with some oil. Cook the egg rolls for 15 minutes on both sides, until the exterior is nice and crispy.
8. Remove them from the grill and enjoy with your favorite salsa!

Nutrition: Carbohydrates: 26.1 g Protein: 9.2 g Fat: 4.2 g Sodium: 373.4 mg Cholesterol: 19.8 mg

Trager Smoked Spatchcock Turkey

Preparation time: 30 minutes
Cooking time: 1 hour 15 minutes
Servings: 8
Ingredients:

- turkey
- 1/2 cup melted butter
- 1/4 cup Blackstone chicken rub
- 1 Tablespoon onion powder
- 1 Tablespoon garlic powder
- 1 Tablespoon rubbed sage

Direction:

1. Preheat your Blackstone to high temperature.
2. Place the turkey on a chopping board with the breast side down and the legs pointing towards you.
3. Cut either side of the turkey backbone, to remove the spine. Flip the turkey and place it on a pan
4. Season both sides with the seasonings and place it on the grill skin side up on the grill.
5. Cook for 30 minutes, reduce temperature, and cook for 45 more minutes or until the internal temperature reaches 1650F.
6. Remove from the Blackstone and let rest for 15 minutes before slicing and serving.

Nutrition: Calories 156, Total fat 16g, Protein 2g, Fiber 0g, Sodium 19mg

Grilled Filet Mignon

Preparation Time: 10 minutes
Cooking Time: 20 minutes
Servings: 1
Ingredients:

- Salt
- Pepper
- Filet mignon - 3

Directions:

1. Preheat your grill to 450 degrees.
2. Season the steak with a good amount of salt and pepper to enhance its flavor.
3. Place on the grill and flip after 5 minutes.
4. Grill both sides for 5 minutes each.
5. Take it out when it looks cooked and serve with your favorite side dish.

Nutrition: Carbohydrates: 0 g Protein: 23 g Fat: 15 g Sodium: 240 mg Cholesterol: 82 mg

Buttery Apple Smoked Turkey

Preparation time: 30 minutes
Cooking Time: 6 Hours
Servings: 1
Ingredients:

- Whole Turkey - 1 (10-lbs., 4.5-kgs)
- The Rub
- Minced garlic – 2 tablespoons
- Salt – 2 ½ tablespoons
- The Filling
- Garlic powder – 1 ½ tablespoons
- Black pepper – 1 ½ tablespoons
- Butter – 1 cup
- Unsweetened apple juice – 1 cup
- Fresh apples – 2
- Chopped onion – 1 cup
- The Fire
- Preheat the smoker an hour prior to smoking.
- Use charcoal and hickory wood chips for smoking.

Directions:

1. Preheat a smoker to 225°F (107°C) with charcoal and hickory wood chips.
2. Rub the turkey with salt and minced garlic then set aside.
3. After that, cut the apples into cubes then combine with garlic powder, black pepper, butter, and chopped onion.
4. Pour the unsweetened apple juice over the filling mixture then mix well.
5. Fill the turkey's cavity with the filling mixture then cover the turkey with aluminum foil.
6. Place in the smoker once the smoker is ready and smoke it for 10 hours or until the internal temperature has reached 180°F (82°C). Don't forget to check the smoke and add more wood chips if it is necessary.
7. When the turkey is done, remove from the smoker then let it sit for a few minutes.
8. Unwrap the turkey then place on a flat surface.
9. Cut the turkey into pieces or slices then serve.
10. Enjoy.

Nutrition: Carbohydrates: 37 g Protein: 9 g Sodium: 565 mg Cholesterol: 49 mg

Smoked Turkey Legs_grill

Preparation Time: 30 minutes
Cooking Time: 6 Hours
Servings: 1
Ingredients:

- 4 turkey legs
- 2 bay leaves
- 1 cup of BBQ rubs
- 1 tablespoon of crushed allspice berries
- 2 teaspoons of liquid smoke
- ½ gal of cold water
- 4 cups of ice
- 1 gal of warm water
- ½ cup of brown sugar
- ½ cup of curing salt
- 1 tablespoon of peppercorns; whole black

Directions:

1. Take a large stockpot and mix a gallon of warm water to curing salt, rub, peppercorns, brown sugar, liquid smoke, allspice and bay leaves
2. Bring this mix to boil by keeping the flame on high heat and let all salt granules dissolve thoroughly
3. Now let it cool to room temperature
4. Now add ice and cold water and let the whole thing chill in the refrigerator
5. Add turkey legs and make sure they are submerged in the brine
6. Let it stay for a day
7. Now drain the turkey legs and get rid of the brine
8. Wash off the brine from the legs with the help of cold water and then pat it dry
9. Set the grill to preheat by keeping the temperature to 250 degrees F
10. Lay the legs directly on the grate of the grill
11. Smoke it for 4 to 5 hours till the internal temperature reaches 165 degrees F
12. Serve and enjoy

Nutrition: Carbohydrates: 39 g Protein: 29 g Sodium: 15 mg Cholesterol: 19 mg

Smoked Turkey in Beer Brine

Preparation time: 30 minutes
Cooking Time: 6 Hours
Servings: 1
Ingredients:

- Whole Turkey - 1 (10-lbs., 4.5-kgs)
- The Brine
- Water – 1 liter
- Salt – 2 cups
- Brown sugar – 1 sugar
- Bay leaves – 3 leaves
- Thyme – 1 cup
- Chopped onion – 1 cup
- Cold beer – 1 gallon
- The Fire
- Preheat the smoker an hour prior to smoking.
- Use charcoal and hickory wood chips for smoking.

Directions:

1. Pour water into a pot then add salt, brown sugar, bay leaves, thyme, and chopped onion. Bring to boil.
2. Once it is boiled, remove from heat and let it cool. Usually, it will take approximately 30 minutes.
3. When the brine is cool, transfer to a container then pour cold beer into it. Mix until incorporated.
4. Add turkey to the container then refrigerate for 24 hours until the turkey is completely seasoned.
5. After 24 hours, remove from the refrigerator and dry using a paper towel. Set aside.
6. Preheat a smoker to 225°F (107°C) with charcoal and hickory wood chips.
7. Place the turkey in the sm0ker then smoke for 6 hours or until the internal temperature has reached 160°F (71°C).
8. Remove the smoked turkey from the smoker then let it warm.
9. Cut the smoked turkey into pieces or slices then arrange on a serving dish.
10. Serve and enjoy.

Nutrition: Carbohydrates: 37 g Protein: 9 g Sodium: 565 mg Cholesterol: 49 mg

Hot Smoked Turkey with Jelly Glaze

Preparation time: 30 minutes
Cooking Time: 6 Hours
Servings: 1
Ingredients:

- Whole Turkey - 1 (10-lbs., 4.5-kgs)
- The Rub
- Olive oil – ½ cup
- Salt – 3 tablespoons
- Pepper – 2 tablespoons
- The Glaze
- Hot pepper jelly – ¾ cup
- Rice vinegar – 3 tablespoons
- Red pepper flakes – ¼ cup

The Fire

- Preheat the smoker an hour prior to smoking.
- Use charcoal and hickory wood chips for smoking.

Directions:

1. Preheat a smoker to 225°F (107°C) with charcoal and hickory wood chips. Wait until the smoker is ready.
2. Cut the excess fat of the turkey then brush all sides of the turkey with olive oil,
3. Sprinkle salt and pepper over the turkey then place it in the smoker.
4. Smoke the turkey for 6 hours or until the internal temperature has reached 160°F (71°C).
5. Meanwhile, combine hot pepper jelly with rice vinegar and red pepper flakes then mix well.
6. After 6 hours, brush the smoked turkey with the hot pepper jelly mixture then return to the smoker.
7. Smoke for about 20 minutes then remove from the smoker.
8. Let the smoked turkey warm for a few minutes then cut into slices.
9. Arrange on a serving dish then serve.
10. Enjoy!

Nutrition: Carbohydrates: 27 g Protein: 19 g Sodium: 65 mg Cholesterol: 49 mg

SMOKING RECIPES

Smoked Ribs

Preparation Time: 20 minutes
Cooking Time: 6 hours
Servings: 8
Ingredients:

- Four baby back ribs
- 1 cup pork rubs
- 1 cup barbecue sauce

Directions:

1. Preheat your grill to 180 tiers F for 15 minutes simultaneously as the lid is closed.
2. Sprinkle toddler again ribs with beef rub.
3. Smoke the ribs for 5 hours.
4. Brush the ribs with barbecue sauce.
5. Wrap the ribs with foil.
6. Put the ribs again on the grill.
7. Increase temperature to 350 levels F.
8. Cook for forty-five minutes to at least one hour.
9. Let rest before slicing and serving.

Nutrition: Energy (calories): 493 kcal Protein: 38.78 g Fat: 30.94 g Carbohydrates: 14.97 g

Smoked Pot Roast

Preparation Time: 30 minutes
Cooking Time: 6 hours
Servings: 4
Ingredients:

- Salt and pepper to taste
- 1 tsp. Onion powder 1 tsp. garlic powder
- 3 lb. chuck roast
- 2 cups potatoes, sliced in half
- 2 cups carrots, sliced
- Two onions, peeled
- 1 tsp. chili powder
- 1 cup red wine
- 1 tbsp. fresh rosemary, chopped
- 1 tbsp. fresh thyme, chopped
- Two dried chipotle peppers
- 2 cups beef stock

Directions:

1. Mix the salt, pepper, onion powder, and garlic powder in a bowl.
2. Rub chuck roast with this aggregate.
3. Preheat your pellet grill to 180 ranges F for 15 minutes while the lid is closed.
4. Smoke the pork for 1 hour.
5. Increase temperature to 275 tiers F.
6. Place the pork and the relaxation of the ingredients in a Dutch oven.
7. Seal the Dutch oven and area on the grill.
8. Braise for five hours.

Nutrition: Energy (calories): 733 kcal Protein: 95.53 g Fat: 29.17 g Carbohydrates: 20.59 g

Smoked Brisket

Preparation Time: 30 minutes
Cooking Time: 12 hours
Servings: 8
Ingredients:

- Salt and pepper to taste
- 2 tbsp. beef rub
- 1 tbsp. Worcestershire sauce
- 6 lb. brisket
- 1 cup beef broth

Directions:

1. Mix salt, pepper, beef rub, and Worcestershire sauce in a bowl.
2. Rub brisket with this combination.
3. Preheat your wood pellet grill to 180 levels F for 15 minutes while the lid is closed.
4. Smoke the brisket for 7 hours.
5. Transfer brisket on top of a foil.
6. Pour the broth over the brisket.
7. Wrap it with foil.
8. Smoke for five hours.
9. Let rest before slicing.

Nutrition: Energy (calories): 464 kcal Protein: 73.34 g Fat: 17.43 g Carbohydrates: 3.54 g

Blackstone Smoked Potatoes

Preparation Time: 30 minutes
Cooking Time: 1 hour
Servings: 6

Ingredients:

- 2 tbsp. butter
- 1/2 cup milk
- 1 cup heavy cream
- Two cloves garlic, crushed and minced
- 2 tbsp. flour
- Four potatoes, sliced thinly
- Salt and pepper to taste
- 1 cup cheddar cheese, grated

Directions:

1. Preheat your wood pellet grill to 375 levels F for 15 minutes at the same time as the lid is closed.
2. Add butter to your forged iron pan.
3. In a bowl, blend the milk, cream, garlic, and flour.
4. Arrange some of the potatoes in a pan.
5. Season with salt and pepper.
6. Pour some of the sauce over the potatoes.
7. Repeat layers till elements were used.
8. Grill for 50 minutes.
9. Sprinkle cheese on top and prepare dinner for 10 minutes.

Nutrition: Energy (calories): 176 kcal Protein: 2.78 g Fat: 12 g Carbohydrates: 15.14 g

FISH AND SEAFOOD RECIPES

Grilled Lobster Tail

Preparation Time: 10 minutes
Cooking Time: 15 minutes
Servings: 4
Ingredients:

- 2 (8 ounces each) lobster tails
- 1/4 tsp old bay seasoning
- ½ tsp oregano
- 1 tsp paprika
- Juice from one lemon
- 1/4 tsp Himalayan salt
- 1/4 tsp freshly ground black pepper
- 1/4 tsp onion powder
- 2 tbsp freshly chopped parsley
- ¼ cup melted butter

Directions:

1. Slice the tail in the middle with a kitchen shear. Pull the shell apart slightly and run your hand through the meat to separate the meat partially
2. Combine the seasonings
3. Drizzle lobster tail with lemon juice and season generously with the seasoning mixture.
4. Preheat your wood pellet smoker to 450°F, using apple wood pellets.
5. Place the lobster tail directly on the grill grate, meat side down. Cook for about 15 minutes.
6. The tails must be pulled off and it must cool down for a few minutes
7. Drizzle melted butter over the tails.
8. Serve and garnish with fresh chopped parsley.

Nutrition: Calories: 146 Cal Fat: 11.7 g Carbohydrates: 2.1 g Protein: 9.3 g Fiber: 0.8 g

Halibut

Preparation Time: 10 minutes
Cooking Time: 3o minutes
Servings: 4
Ingredients:

- 1-pound fresh halibut filet (cut into 4 equal sizes)
- 1 tbsp fresh lemon juice
- 2 garlic cloves (minced)
- 2 tsp soy sauce
- ½ tsp ground black pepper
- ½ tsp onion powder
- 2 tbsp honey
- ½ tsp oregano
- 1 tsp dried basil
- 2 tbsp butter (melted)
- Maple syrup for serving

Directions:

1. Combine the lemon juice, honey, soy sauce, onion powder, oregano, dried basil, pepper and garlic.
2. Brush the halibut filets generously with the filet the mixture. Wrap the filets with aluminum foil and refrigerate for 4 hours.
3. Remove the filets from the refrigerator and let them sit for about 2 hours, or until they are at room temperature.
4. Activate your wood pellet grill on smoke, leaving the lid opened for 5 minutes or until fire starts.
5. The lid must not be opened for it to be preheated and reach 275°F 15 minutes, using fruit wood pellets.
6. Place the halibut filets directly on the grill grate and smoke for 30 minutes
7. Remove the filets from the grill and let them rest for 10 minutes.
8. Serve and top with maple syrup to taste

Nutrition: Calories: 180 Cal Fat: 6.3 g Carbohydrates: 10 g Protein: 20.6 g Fiber: 0.3 g

Grilled Salmon
Preparation Time: 10 minutes
Cooking Time: 4o minutes
Servings: 8
Ingredients:

- 2 pounds salmon (cut into fillets)
- 1/2 cup low sodium soy sauce
- 2 garlic cloves (grated)
- 4 tbsp olive oil
- 2 tbsp honey
- 1 tsp ground black pepper
- ½ tsp smoked paprika
- ½ tsp Italian seasoning
- 2 tbsp chopped green onion

Directions:

1. Incorporate pepper, paprika, Italian seasoning, garlic, soy sauce and olive oil. Add the salmon fillets and toss to combine. Cover the bowl and refrigerate for 1 hour.
2. Remove the fillets from the marinade and let it sit for about 2 hours, or until it is at room temperature.
3. Start the wood pellet on smoke, leaving the lid opened for 5 minutes, or until fire starts.
4. Keep lid unopened and preheat grill to a temperature 350°F for 15 minutes.
5. Do not open lid for 4 minutes or until cooked
6. Flip the fillets and cook for additional 25 minutes or until the fish is flaky.
7. Remove the fillets from heat and let it sit for a few minutes.
8. Serve warm and garnish with chopped green onion.

Nutrition: Calories: 317 Cal Fat: 18.8 g Carbohydrates: 8.3 g Protein: 30.6 g Fiber: 0.4 g

Barbeque Shrimp

Preparation Time: 20 minutes
Cooking Time: 8 minutes
Servings: 6
Ingredients:

- 2-pound raw shrimp (peeled and deveined)
- ¼ cup extra virgin olive oil
- ½ tsp paprika
- ½ tsp red pepper flakes
- 2 garlic cloves (minced)
- 1 tsp cumin
- 1 lemon (juiced)
- 1 tsp kosher salt
- 1 tbsp chili paste
- Bamboo or wooden skewers (soaked for 30 minutes, at least)

Directions:

1. Combine the pepper flakes, cumin, lemon, salt, chili, paprika, garlic and olive oil. Add the shrimp and toss to combine.
2. Transfer the shrimp and marinade into a zip-lock bag and refrigerate for 4 hours.
3. Let shrimp rest in room temperature after pulling it out from marinade
4. Start your grill on smoke, leaving the lid opened for 5 minutes, or until fire starts. Use hickory wood pellet.
5. Keep lid unopened and preheat the grill to "high" for 15 minutes.
6. Thread shrimps onto skewers and arrange the skewers on the grill grate.
7. Smoke shrimps for 8 minutes, 4 minutes per side.
8. Serve and enjoy.

Nutrition: Calories: 267 Cal Fat: 11.6 g Carbohydrates: 4.9 g Protein: 34.9 g Fiber: 0.4 g

Blackstone Grilled Tuna steaks

Preparation Time: 5 minutes
Cooking Time: 4 minutes
Servings: 4
Ingredients:

- 4 (6 ounce each) tuna steaks (1 inch thick)
- 1 lemon (juiced)
- 1 clove garlic (minced)
- 1 tsp chili
- 2 tbsp extra virgin olive oil
- 1 cup white wine
- 3 tbsp brown sugar
- 1 tsp rosemary

Directions:

1. Combine lemon, chili, white wine, sugar, rosemary, olive oil and garlic. Add the tuna steaks and toss to combine.
2. Transfer the tuna and marinade to a zip-lock bag. Refrigerate for 3 hours.
3. Remove the tuna steaks from the marinade and let them rest for about 1 hour
4. Start your grill on smoke, leaving the lid opened for 5 minutes, or until fire starts.
5. Do not open lid to preheat until 15 minutes to the setting "HIGH"
6. Grease the grill grate with oil and place the tuna on the grill grate. Grill tuna steaks for 4 minutes, 2 minutes per side.
7. Remove the tuna from the grill and let them rest for a few minutes.

Nutrition: Calories: 137 Cal Fat: 17.8 g Carbohydrates: 10.2 g Protein: 51.2 g Fiber: 0.6 g

Oyster in Shells

Preparation Time: 25 minutes
Cooking Time: 8 minutes
Servings: 4
Ingredients:

- 12 medium oysters
- 1 tsp oregano
- 1 lemon (juiced)
- 1 tsp freshly ground black pepper
- 6 tbsp unsalted butter (melted)
- 1 tsp salt or more to taste
- 2 garlic cloves (minced)
- 2 ½ tbsp grated parmesan cheese
- 2 tbsp freshly chopped parsley

Directions:

1. Remove dirt
2. Open the shell completely. Discard the top shell.
3. Gently run the knife under the oyster to loosen the oyster foot from the bottom shell.
4. Repeat step 2 and 3 for the remaining oysters.
5. Combine melted butter, lemon, pepper, salt, garlic and oregano in a mixing bowl.
6. Pour ½ to 1 tsp of the butter mixture on each oyster.
7. Start your wood pellet grill on smoke, leaving the lid opened for 5 minutes, or until fire starts.
8. Keep lid unopened to preheat in the set "HIGH" with lid closed for 15 minutes.
9. Gently arrange the oysters onto the grill grate.
10. Grill oyster for 6 to 8 minutes or until the oyster juice is bubbling and the oyster is plump.
11. Remove oysters from heat. Serve and top with grated parmesan and chopped parsley.

Nutrition: Calories: 200 Cal Fat: 19.2 g Carbohydrates: 3.9 g Protein: 4.6 g Fiber: 0.8 g

Grilled King Crab Legs

Preparation Time: 10 minutes
Cooking Time: 25 minutes
Servings: 4
Ingredients:

- 4 pounds king crab legs (split)
- 4 tbsp lemon juice
- 2 tbsp garlic powder
- 1 cup butter (melted)
- 2 tsp brown sugar
- 2 tsp paprika
- Black pepper (depends to your liking)

Directions:

1. In a mixing bowl, combine the lemon juice, butter, sugar, garlic, paprika and pepper.
2. Arrange the split crab on a baking sheet, split side up.
3. Drizzle ¾ of the butter mixture over the crab legs.
4. Configure your pellet grill for indirect cooking and preheat it to 225°F, using mesquite wood pellets.
5. Arrange the crab legs onto the grill grate, shell side down.
6. Cover the grill and cook 25 minutes.
7. Remove the crab legs from the grill.
8. Serve and top with the remaining butter mixture.

Nutrition: Calories: 480 Cal Fat: 53.2 g Carbohydrates: 6.1 g Protein: 88.6 g Fiber: 1.2 g

Cajun Smoked Catfish

Preparation Time: 15 minutes
Cooking Time: 2 hours
Servings: 4
Ingredients:

- 4 catfish fillets (5 ounces each)
- ½ cup Cajun seasoning
- 1 tsp ground black pepper
- 1 tbsp smoked paprika
- 1/4 tsp cayenne pepper
- 1 tsp hot sauce
- 1 tsp granulated garlic
- 1 tsp onion powder
- 1 tsp thyme
- 1 tsp salt or more to taste
- 2 tbsp chopped fresh parsley

Directions:

1. Pour water into the bottom of a square or rectangular dish. Add 4 tbsp salt. Arrange the catfish fillets into the dish. Cover the dish and refrigerate for 3 to 4 hours.
2. Combine the paprika, cayenne, hot sauce, onion, salt, thyme, garlic, pepper and Cajun seasoning in a mixing bowl.
3. Remove the fish from the dish and let it sit for a few minutes, or until it is at room temperature. Pat the fish fillets dry with a paper towel.
4. Rub the seasoning mixture over each fillet generously.
5. Start your grill on smoke, leaving the lid opened for 5 minutes, or until fire starts.
6. Keep lid unopened and preheat to 200°F, using mesquite hardwood pellets.
7. Arrange the fish fillets onto the grill grate and close the grill. Cook for about 2 hours, or until the fish is flaky.
8. Remove the fillets from the grill and let the fillets rest for a few minutes to cool.
9. Serve and garnish with chopped fresh parsley.

Nutrition: Calories: 204 Cal Fat: 11.1 g Carbohydrates: 2.7 g Protein: 22.9 g Fiber: 0.6 g

Smoked Scallops

Preparation Time: 10 minutes
Cooking Time: 15 minutes
Servings: 6
Ingredients:

- 2 pounds sea scallops
- 4 tbsp salted butter
- 2 tbsp lemon juice
- ½ tsp ground black pepper
- 1 garlic clove (minced)
- 1 kosher tsp salt
- 1 tsp freshly chopped tarragon

Directions:

1. Let the scallops dry using paper towels and drizzle all sides with salt and pepper to season
2. Place you're a cast iron pan in your grill and preheat the grill to 400°F with lid closed for 15 minutes.
3. Combine the butter and garlic in hot cast iron pan. Add the scallops and stir. Close grill lid and cook for 8 minutes.
4. Flip the scallops and cook for an additional 7 minutes.
5. Remove the scallop from heat and let it rest for a few minutes.
6. Stir in the chopped tarragon. Serve and top with lemon juice.

Nutrition: Calories: 204 Cal Fat: 8.9 g Carbohydrates: 4 g Protein: 25.6 g Fiber: 0.1 g

Grilled Tilapia

Preparation Time: 10 minutes
Cooking Time: 2o minutes
Servings: 6
Ingredients:

- 2 tsp dried parsley
- ½ tsp garlic powder
- 1 tsp cayenne pepper
- ½ tsp ground black pepper
- ½ tsp thyme
- ½ tsp dried basil
- ½ tsp oregano
- 3 tbsp olive oil
- ½ tsp lemon pepper
- 1 tsp kosher salt
- 1 lemon (juiced)
- 6 tilapia fillets
- 1 ½ tsp creole seafood seasoning

Directions:

1. In a mixing bowl, combine spices
2. Brush the fillets with oil and lemon juice.
3. Liberally, season all sides of the tilapia fillets with the seasoning mix.
4. Preheat your grill to 325°F
5. Place a non-stick BBQ grilling try on the grill and arrange the tilapia fillets onto it.
6. Grill for 15 to 20 minutes
7. Remove fillets and cool down

Nutrition: Calories: 176 Cal Fat: 9.6 g Carbohydrates: 1.5 g Protein: 22.3 g Fiber: 0.5 g

Blackstone Salmon with Togarashi

Preparation Time: 5 Minutes
Cooking Time: 20 Minutes
Servings: 3
Ingredients:

- One salmon fillet
- 1/4 cup olive oil
- 1/2 tbsp kosher salt
- 1 tbsp Togarashi seasoning

Directions:

1. Preheat your Blackstone to 4000F.
2. Place the salmon on a sheet lined with non-stick foil with the skin side down.
3. Rub the oil into the meat, then sprinkle salt and Togarashi.
4. Place the salmon on the grill and cook for 20 minutes or until the internal temperature reaches 1450F with the lid closed.
5. Remove from the Blackstone and serve when hot.

Nutrition: Calories 119Total fat 10g Saturated fat 2g Sodium 720mg

VEGETARIAN RECIPES

Kale Chips

Preparation Time: 30 Minutes
Cooking Time: 20 Minutes
Servings: 4
Ingredients:

- 4 cups kale leaves
- Olive oil
- Salt to taste

Directions:

1. Drizzle kale with oil and sprinkle it with salt.
2. Set the Blackstone wood pellet grill to 250 degrees F.
3. Preheat it for 15 minutes while the lid is closed.
4. Add the kale leaves to a baking pan.
5. Place the pan on the grill.
6. Cook the kale for 20 minutes or until crispy.

Nutrition: Calories 118 Total fat 7.6g Total carbs 10.8g Protein 5.4g, Sugars 3.7g Fiber 2.5g, Sodium 3500mg Potassium 536mg

Sweet Potato Fries

Preparation Time: 30 Minutes
Cooking Time: 40 Minutes
Servings: 4
Ingredients:

- Three sweet potatoes, sliced into strips
- Four tablespoons olive oil
- Two tablespoons fresh rosemary, chopped
- Salt and pepper to taste

Directions:

1. Set the Blackstone wood pellet grill to 450 degrees F.
2. Preheat it for 10 minutes.
3. Spread the sweet potato strips in the baking pan.
4. Toss in olive oil and sprinkle with rosemary, salt, and pepper.
5. Cook for 15 minutes.
6. Flip and cook for another 15 minutes.
7. Flip and cook for ten more minutes.

Nutrition: Calories 118 Total fat 7.6g Total carbs 10.8g Protein 5.4g Sugars 3.7g Fiber 2.5g, Sodium 3500mg Potassium 536mg

Potato Fries with Chipotle Peppers

Preparation Time: 30 Minutes
Cooking Time: 30 Minutes
Servings: 4
Ingredients:

- Four potatoes, sliced into strips
- Three tablespoons olive oil
- Salt and pepper to taste
- 1 cup mayonnaise
- Two chipotle peppers in adobo sauce
- Two tablespoons lime juice

Directions:

1. Set the Blackstone wood pellet grill to high.
2. Preheat it for 15 minutes while the lid is closed.
3. Coat the potato strips with oil.
4. Sprinkle with salt and pepper.
5. Put a baking pan on the grate.
6. Transfer potato strips to the pan.
7. Cook potatoes until crispy.
8. Mix the remaining ingredients.
9. Pulse in a food processor until pureed.
10. Serve potato fries with chipotle dip.

Nutrition: Calories 118 Total fat 7.6g Total carbs 10.8g Protein 5.4g Sugars 3.7g Fiber 2.5g, Sodium 3500mg Potassium 536mg

Blackstone Grilled Zucchini

Preparation Time: 30 Minutes
Cooking Time: 10 Minutes
Servings: 4
Ingredients:

- Four zucchinis, sliced into strips
- One tablespoon sherry vinegar
- Two tablespoons olive oil
- Salt and pepper to taste
- Two fresh thyme, chopped

Directions:

1. Place the zucchini strips in a bowl.
2. Mix the remaining fixings and pour them into the zucchini.
3. Coat evenly.
4. Set the Blackstone wood pellet grill to 350 degrees F.
5. Preheat for 15 minutes while the lid is closed.
6. Place the zucchini on the grill.
7. Cook for 3 minutes per side.

Nutrition: Calories 118 Total fat 7.6g Total carbs 10.8g Protein 5.4g Sugars 3.7g Fiber 2.5g, Sodium 3500mg Potassium 536mg

Smoked Potato Salad

Preparation Time: 1 Hour and 15 Minutes

Cooking Time: 40 Minutes

Servings: 4

Ingredients:

- 2 lb. potatoes
- Two tablespoons olive oil
- 2 cups mayonnaise
- One tablespoon white wine vinegar
- One tablespoon dry mustard
- 1/2 onion, chopped
- Two celery stalks, chopped
- Salt and pepper to taste

Directions:

1. Coat the potatoes with oil.
2. Smoke the potatoes in the Blackstone wood pellet grill at 180 degrees F for 20 minutes.
3. Increase temperature to 450 degrees F and cook for 20 more minutes.
4. Transfer to a bowl and let cool.
5. Peel potatoes.
6. Slice into cubes.
7. Refrigerate for 30 minutes.
8. Stir in the rest of the ingredients.

Nutrition: Calories 118 Total fat 7.6g Total carbs 10.8g Protein 5.4g Sugars 3.7g Fiber 2.5g, Sodium 3500mg Potassium 536mg

Baked Parmesan Mushrooms

Preparation Time: 15 Minutes
Cooking Time: 15 Minutes
Servings: 8
Ingredients:

- Eight mushroom caps
- 1/2 cup Parmesan cheese, grated
- 1/2 teaspoon garlic salt
- 1/4 cup mayonnaise
- Pinch paprika
- Hot sauce

Directions:

1. Place mushroom caps in a baking pan.
2. Mix the remaining ingredients in a bowl.
3. Scoop the mixture onto the mushroom.
4. Place the baking pan on the grill.
5. Cook in the Blackstone wood pellet grill at 350 degrees F for 15 minutes while the lid isclosed.

Nutrition: Calories 118 Total fat 7.6g Total carbs 10.8g Protein 5.4g Sugars 3.7g Fiber 2.5g, Sodium 3500mg Potassium 536mg

Roasted Spicy Tomatoes

Preparation Time: 30 Minutes
Cooking Time: 1 Hour and 30 Minutes
Servings: 4
Ingredients:

- 2 lb. large tomatoes, sliced in half
- Olive oil
- Two tablespoons garlic, chopped
- Three tablespoons parsley, chopped
- Salt and pepper to taste
- Hot pepper sauce

Directions:

1. Set the temperature to 400 degrees F.
2. Preheat it for 15 minutes while the lid is closed.
3. Add tomatoes to a baking pan.
4. Drizzle with oil and sprinkle with garlic, parsley, salt, and pepper.
5. Roast for 1 hour and 30 minutes.
6. Drizzle with hot pepper sauce and serve.

Nutrition: Calories 118 Total fat 7.6g Total carbs 10.8g Protein 5.4g Sugars 3.7g Fiber 2.5g, Sodium 3500mg Potassium 536mg

VEGAN RECIPES

Wood Pellet Smoked Mushrooms

Preparation Time: 15 minutes,
Cooking Time: 45 minutes.
Servings: 5

Ingredients:

- 4 cup Portobello, whole and cleaned
- 1 tbsp. canola oil
- 1 tbsp. onion powder
- 1 tbsp. granulated garlic
- 1 tbsp. salt
- 1 tbsp. pepper

Directions:

1. Put all the ingredients and mix well.
2. Set the wood pellet temperature to 180°F then place the mushrooms directly on the grill.
3. Smoke the mushrooms for 30 minutes.
4. Increase the temperature to high and cook the mushrooms for a further 15 minutes.
5. Serve and enjoy.

Nutrition: Calories: 1680 Fat: 30g Carbs: 10g Protein: 4g Sodium: 514mg, Potassium: 0mg:

Wood Pellet Grilled Zucchini Squash Spears

Preparation Time: 5 minutes,
Cooking Time: 10 minutes.
Servings: 5

Ingredients:

- 4 zucchinis, cleaned and ends cut
- 2 tbsp. olive oil
- 1 tbsp. sherry vinegar
- 2 thyme leaves pulled
- Salt and pepper to taste

Directions:

1. Cut the zucchini into halves then cut each half thirds.
2. Add the rest of the ingredients in a zip lock bag with the zucchini pieces. Toss to mix well.
3. Preheat the wood pellet temperature to 350°F with the lid closed for 15 minutes.
4. Remove the zucchini from the bag and place them on the grill grate with the cut side down.
5. Cook for 4 minutes until the zucchini are tender
6. Remove from grill and serve with thyme leaves. Enjoy.

Nutrition: Calories: 74 Fat: 5.4g Carbs: 6.1g Protein: 2.6g Sugar: 3.9g Fiber: 2.3g Sodium: 302mg Potassium: 599mg:

RED MEAT RECIPES

Chipotle Honey Smoked Beef Roast

Preparation Time: 10 minutes
Cooking Time: 4 hours 20 minutes
Servings: 10

Ingredients:

- Beef roast (5-lbs., 2.3-kg.)
- The Rub Vegetable oil – 2 tablespoons
- Black pepper – 1 ½ tbsp.
- Salt – 1 ½ tbsp.
- Brown sugar – ¾ tablespoon
- Onion powder – ¾ tablespoon
- Mustard – 1 teaspoon
- Garlic powder – 1 ½ tsp.
- Chipotle powder – 1 ½ tsp.
- The Glaze Honey – ½ cup
- Water – 2 tablespoons
- Minced garlic – 1 ½ tbsp.

The Heat

- Hickory wood pellets

Directions:

1. Place the rub ingredients—vegetable oil, black pepper, salt, brown sugar, onion powder, mustard, garlic powder, and chipotle powder in a bowl, and then mix until combined.
2. Rub the beef roast with the spice mixture, and then set aside. Plug the wood pellet smoker and place the wood pellet inside the hopper.
3. Turn the switch on. Set the "Smoke" setting and prepare the wood pellet smoker for indirect heat.
4. Wait until the smoke is ready and adjust the temperature to 275 degrees F (135°C). Once the wood pellet smoker has reached the desired temperature, place the seasoned beef roast directly on the grate inside the wood pellet smoker and smoke for 2 hours.
5. In the meantime, combine honey, water, and minced garlic in a bowl, then stir until incorporated. After 2 hours, take the beef roast out of the wood pellet smoker and place it on a sheet of aluminum foil.
6. Leave the wood pellet smoker on and adjust the temperature to 300 degrees F (149°C). Baste the beef roast with the glaze mixture, and then wrap it with the aluminum foil. Return the wrapped beef roast to the wood pellet smoker, then smoke for another 2 hours.

7. Once the smoked beef roast's internal temperature has reached 165degrees F (74°C), remove it from the wood pellet smoker.
8. Let the smoked beef roast rest for about 10 minutes, then unwrap it. Transfer the smoked beef roast to a serving dish, then serve. Enjoy!

Nutrition: Energy (calories): 324 kcal Protein: 27.7 g Fat: 13.23 g Carbohydrates: 26.4 g

Lemon Chili Smoked Beef Brisket

Preparation Time: 10 minutes
Cooking Time: 4 hours 10 minutes
Servings: 10

Ingredients:

- Beef brisket (4.5-lbs., 2-kg.)
- The Rub Lemon juice – 3 tablespoons
- Chili powder – ¼ cup
- Salt – 1 ½ tbsp.
- Garlic powder – 2 tablespoons
- Cayenne – 2 teaspoons
- Pepper – 2 teaspoons

The Heat

- Alder wood pellets

Directions:

1. Combine chili powder with salt, garlic powder, cayenne, and pepper, and then mix well. Rub the beef brisket with lemon juice, and then sprinkle the dry spice mixture over the beef brisket.
2. Plug the wood pellet smoker and fill the hopper with wood pellets. Turn the switch on. Set the "Smoke" setting and prepare the wood pellet smoker for indirect heat.
3. Adjust the wood pellet smoker's temperature to 275degrees F (135°C) and wait until it reaches the desired temperature. Place the seasoned beef brisket directly on the grate in the wood pellet smoker and smoke for approximately 3 hours or until the internal temperature has reached 125degrees F (52°C).
4. After 2 hours, take the beef brisket out of the wood pellet smoker and transfer it to a sheet of aluminum foil. Wrap the beef brisket with the aluminum foil, and then return it to the wood pellet smoker.
5. Smoke the wrapped beef brisket for another 2 hours or until the internal temperature has reached 165degrees F (74°C). Once it is done, remove the wrapped smoked beef brisket from the wood pellet smoker and let it rest for about 10 minutes.
6. Unwrap the smoked beef brisket, and then cut into slices.
7. Serve and enjoy.

Nutrition: Energy (calories): 425 kcal Protein: 30.96 g Fat: 30.98 g Carbohydrates: 4.66 g

BAKING RECIPES

Quick Yeast Dinner Rolls

Preparation Time: 5 minutes
Cooking Time: 30 minutes
Servings 8
Ingredients:

- 2 tablespoons yeast, quick rise
- 1 cup water, lukewarm
- 3 cups flour
- ¼ cup sugar
- 1 teaspoon salt
- ¼ cup unsalted butter, softened
- 1 egg
- Cooking spray, as needed
- 1 egg, for egg wash

Directions:

1. Combine the yeast and warm water in a small bowl to activate the yeast. Let sit for about 5 to 10 minutes, or until foamy.
2. Combine the flour, sugar, and salt in the bowl of a stand mixer fitted with the dough hook. Pour the water and yeast into the dry ingredients with the machine running on low speed.
3. Add the butter and egg and mix for 10 minutes, gradually increasing the speed from low to high.
4. Form the dough into a ball and place in a buttered bowl. Cover with a cloth and let the dough rise for approximately 40 minutes.
5. Transfer the risen dough to a lightly floured work surface and divide into 8 pieces, forming a ball with each.
6. Lightly spritz a cast iron pan with cooking spray and arrange the balls in the pan. Cover with a cloth and let rise for 20 minutes.
7. When ready to cook, set Blackstone temperature to 375 F (191 C) and preheat, lid closed for 15 minutes.
8. Brush the rolls with the egg wash. Place the pan on the grill and bake for 30 minutes, or until lightly browned.
9. Remove from the grill. Serve hot.

Baked Cornbread with Honey Butter

Preparation Time: 10 minutes
Cooking Time: 35 to 45 minutes
Servings 6
Ingredients:
- 4 ears whole corn
- 1 cup all-purpose flour
- 1 cup cornmeal
- 2/3 cup white sugar
- 1½ teaspoons baking powder
- ½ teaspoon baking soda
- ½ teaspoon salt
- 1 cup buttermilk
- ½ cup butter, softened
- 2 eggs
- ½ cup butter, softened
- ¼ cup honey

Directions:

1. When ready to cook, set Blackstone temperature to High and preheat, lid closed for 15minutes.
2. Peel back the outer layer of the corn husk, keeping it attached to the cob. Remove the silk from the corn and place the husk back into place. Soak the corn in cold water for 10 minutes.
3. Place the corn directly on the grill grate and cook for 15 to 20 minutes, or until the kernels are tender, stirring occasionally. Remove from the grill and set aside.
4. In a large bowl, stir together the flour, cornmeal, sugar, baking powder, baking soda and salt.
5. In a separate bowl, whisk together the buttermilk, butter, and eggs. Pour the wet mixture into the cornmeal mixture and fold together until there are no dry spots. Pour the batter into a greased baking dish.
6. Cut the kernels from the corn and sprinkle over the top of the batter, pressing the kernels down with a spoon to submerge.
7. Turn Blackstone temperature down to 350 F (177 C). Place the baking dish on the grill. Bake for about 20 to 25 minutes, or until the top is golden brown and a toothpick inserted into the middle of the cornbread comes out clean.
8. Remove the cornbread from the grill and let cool for 10 minutes before serving.
9. To make the honey butter, mix the butter and honey until combined. Serve the cornbread with the honey butter.

S'mores Dip with Candied Pecans

Preparation Time: 10 minutes
Cooking Time: 37 to 45 minutes
Servings 4
Ingredients:
Candied Smoked Pecans:

- ½ cup sugar
- ½ cup brown sugar
- 1 tablespoon ground cinnamon
- 1 teaspoon salt
- ¼ teaspoon cayenne pepper
- 1 egg white
- 1 teaspoon water
- 1-pound (454 g) pecans

S'mores Dip:

- 1 tablespoon butter
- 2 cups milk chocolate chips
- 10 large marshmallows, cut in half
- Graham crackers, for serving

Directions:

1. When ready to cook, set Blackstone temperature to 300 F (149 C) and preheat, lid closedfor 15 minutes.
2. In a small bowl, stir together the sugars, cinnamon, salt, and cayenne pepper. In a medium bowl, whisk together the egg white and water until frothy.
3. Pour the pecans into a large bowl. Pour in the egg white mixture and sugar mixture and toss to coat well.
4. Spread the coated pecans on a sheet tray lined with parchment paper. Place the tray directly on the grill grate. Smoke for 30 to 35 minutes, stirring often.
5. Remove from the grill and let cool. Break apart and roughly chop. Set aside.
6. When ready to cook, set Blackstone temperature to 400 F (204 C) and preheat, lid closedfor 15 minutes.
7. Place a cast iron skillet directly on the grill grate while the grill heats up.
8. When the cast iron skillet is hot, melt the butter in the skillet and swirl around the skillet to coat.
9. Add the chocolate chips to the skillet, then top with the marshmallows. Cook for 7 to 10 minutes, or until the chocolate is melted and marshmallows are lightly browned. Remove from the grill.

Spread a handful of the candied pecans over the

CHEESE AND BREAD

Blackstone-Grill Flatbread Pizza

Preparation Time: 10 minutes
Cooking Time: 20 minutes
Servings: 3
Ingredients

Dough

- 2 cups flour
- 1 tbsp salt
- 1 tbsp sugar
- 2 tbsp yeast
- 6 oz warm water

Toppings

- Green/red bell pepper
- 1/2 garlic
- zucchini
- 1/2 onion
- Olive oil
- 5 bacon strips
- 1 cup halved yellow cherry tomatoes
- Sliced jalapenos
- Sliced green olives
- Sliced kalamata olives
- Goat cheese
- For drizzling: Balsamic vinegar

Directions:

1. Combine all dough ingredients in a stand mixer bowl. Mix until the dough is smooth and elastic. Divide into 3 equal balls. Roll each dough ball with a rolling pin into a thin round enough to fit a 12-inch skillet.

2. Grease the skillet using olive oil.
3. Meanwhile, turn your Blackstone grill on smoke for about 4-5 minutes with the lid open. Turn to high and preheat for about 10-15 minutes with the lid closed.
4. Once ready, arrange peppers, garlic, zucchini, and onion on the grill grate then drizzle with oil and salt. Check at 10 minutes.
5. Now remove zucchini from the grill and add bacon. Continue to cook for another 10 minutes until bacon is done.
6. Transfer the toppings on a chopping board to cool. Chop tomatoes, jalapenos and olive.
7. Brush your crust with oil and smash garlic with a fork over the crust. Smear carefully not to tear the crust.
8. Add toppings to the crust in the skillet.
9. Place the skillet on the grill and cook for about 20 minutes until brown edges.
10. Repeat for the other crusts.
11. Now drizzle each with vinegar and slice.
12. Serve and enjoy.

Nutrition: Calories 342, Total fat 1.2g, Saturated fat 0.2g, Total carbs 70.7g, Net carbs 66.8g, Protein 11.7g, Sugars 4.2g, Fiber 3.9g, Sodium 2333mg, Potassium 250mg

Blackstone Smoked Nut Mix

Preparation Time: 15 minutes
Cooking Time: 20 minutes
Servings: 8
Ingredients

- 3 cups mixed nuts (pecans, peanuts, almonds etc.)
- 1/2 tbsp brown sugar
- 1 tbsp thyme, dried
- 1/4 tbsp mustard powder
- 1 tbsp olive oil, extra-virgin

Directions:

1. Preheat your Blackstone grill to 250oF with the lid closed for about 15 minutes.
2. Combine all ingredients in a bowl, large, then transfer into a cookie sheet lined with parchment paper.
3. Place the cookie sheet on a grill and grill for about 20 minutes.
4. Remove the nuts from the grill and let cool.
5. Serve and enjoy.

Nutrition: Calories 249, Total fat 21.5g, Saturated fat 3.5g, Total carbs 12.3g, Net carbs 10.1g, Protein 5.7g, Sugars 5.6g, Fiber 2.1g, Sodium 111mg, Potassium 205mg

APPETIZERS AND SIDES

Atomic Buffalo Turds

Preparation Time: 30 to 45 Minutes
Cooking Time: 1.5 Hours to 2 Hours
Servings: 6
Ingredients:

- 10 Medium Jalapeno Pepper
- 8 ounces regular cream cheese at room temperature
- ¾ Cup Monterey Jack and Cheddar Cheese Blend Shred (optional)
- One teaspoon smoked paprika
- One teaspoon garlic powder
- ½ teaspoon cayenne pepper
- Teaspoon red pepper flakes (optional)
- 20 smoky sausages
- Ten sliced bacon, cut in half

Directions:

1. Wear food service gloves when using. Jalapeno peppers are washed vertically and sliced. Carefully remove seeds and veins using a spoon or paring knife and discard. Place Jalapeno on a grilled vegetable tray and set aside.
2. A small bowl, mix cream cheese, shredded cheese, paprika, garlic powder, cayenne pepper is used, and red pepper flakes if used until thoroughly mixed.
3. Mix cream cheese with half of the jalapeno pepper.
4. Place the Little Smokiness sausage on half of the filled jalapeno pepper.
5. Wrap half of the thin bacon around half of each jalapeno peppers.
6. Fix the bacon to the sausage with a toothpick so that the pepper does not pierce. Place the ABT on the grill tray or pan.
7. Set the wood pellet smoker and grill for indirect cooking and preheat to 250 degrees Fahrenheit using hickory pellets or blends.
8. Suck jalapeno peppers at 250 ° F for about 1.5 to 2 hours until the bacon is cooked and crisp.
9. Remove the ABT from the grill and let it rest for 5 minutes before hors d'oeuvres.

Nutrition: Calories: 131 Carbs: 1g Fat: 12g Protein: 5g

Grilled Corn

Preparation Time: 15 minutes
Cooking Time: 25 minutes
Servings: 6
Ingredients:

- Six fresh ears of corn
- Salt
- Black pepper
- Olive oil
- Vegetable seasoning
- Butter for serving

Directions:

1. Preheat the grill to high with a closed lid.
2. Peel the husks. Remove the corn's silk. Rub with black pepper, salt, vegetable seasoning, and oil.
3. Close the husks and grill for 25 minutes. Turn them occasionally.
4. Serve topped with butter and enjoy.

Nutrition: Calories: 70 Protein: 3g Carbs: 18g Fat: 2g

Thyme - Rosemary Mash Potatoes

Preparation Time: 20 minutes
Cooking Time: 1 hour
Servings: 6
Ingredients:

- 4 ½ lbs. Potatoes, russet
- Salt
- 1 pint of Heavy cream
- 3 Thyme sprigs + 2 tablespoons for garnish
- 2 Rosemary sprigs
- 6 - 7 Sage leaves
- 6 - 7 Black peppercorns
- Black pepper to taste
- Two stick Butter softened
- 2 Garlic cloves, chopped

Directions:

1. Preheat the grill to 350F with a closed lid.
2. Peel the russet potatoes.
3. Cut into small pieces and place them in a baking dish. Fill it with water (1 ½ cups). Place on the grill and cook with a closed lid for about 1 hour.
4. In the meantime, in a saucepan, combine the garlic, peppercorns, herbs, and cream. Place on the grate and cook covered for about 15 minutes. Once done, strain to remove the garlic and herbs. Keep warm.
5. Take out the water of the potatoes and place them in a stockpot. Rice them with a fork and pour 2/3 of the mixture. Add one stick of softened butter and salt.
6. Serve right away.

Nutrition: Calories: 180 Protein: 4g Carbs: 28g Fat: 10g

MORE SIDES

Grilled Mushroom Skewers
Preparation Time: 5 Minutes
Cooking Time: 60 Minutes
Servings: 6
Ingredients:

- 16 - oz 1 lb. Baby Portobello Mushrooms

For the marinade:

- ¼ - cup olive oil
- ¼ - cup lemon juice
- Small handful of parsley
- 1 - tsp sugar
- 1 - tsp salt
- ¼ - tsp pepper
- ¼ - tsp cayenne pepper
- 1 to 2 - garlic cloves
- 1 - Tbsp balsamic vinegar

What you will need:

- 10 - inch bamboo/wood skewers

Directions:

1. Add the beans to the plate of a lipped container, in an even layer. Shower the softened spread uniformly out ludicrous, and utilizing a couple of tongs tenderly hurl the beans with the margarine until all around covered.
2. Season the beans uniformly, and generously, with salt and pepper.
3. Preheat the smoker to 275 degrees. Include the beans, and smoke 3-4 hours, hurling them like clockwork or until delicate wilted, and marginally seared in spots.
4. Spot 10 medium sticks into a heating dish and spread with water. It's critical to douse the sticks for in any event 15 minutes (more is better) or they will consume too rapidly on the flame broil.
5. Spot the majority of the marinade fixings in a nourishment processor and heartbeat a few times until marinade is almost smooth.
6. Flush your mushrooms and pat dry. Cut each mushroom down the middle, so each piece has half of the mushroom stem.
7. Spot the mushroom parts into an enormous gallon-size Ziploc sack, or a medium bowl and pour in the marinade. Shake the pack until the majority of the mushrooms are equally covered in marinade. Refrigerate and marinate for 30mins to 45mins.
8. Preheat your barbecue about 300F

9. Stick the mushrooms cozily onto the bamboo/wooden sticks that have been dousing (no compelling reason to dry the sticks). Piercing the mushrooms was a bit of irritating from the outset until I got the hang of things.
10. I've discovered that it's least demanding to stick them by bending them onto the stick. In the event that you simply drive the stick through, it might make the mushroom break.
11. Spot the pierced mushrooms on the hot barbecue for around 3mins for every side, causing sure the mushrooms don't consume to the flame broil. The mushrooms are done when they are delicate; as mushrooms ought to be Remove from the barbecue. Spread with foil to keep them warm until prepared to serve

Nutrition: Calories: 230 Carbs: 10g Fat: 20g Protein: 5g

Caprese Tomato Salad

Preparation Time: 5 Minutes
Cooking Time: 60 Minutes
Servings: 4
Ingredients:

- 3 - cups halved multicolored cherry tomatoes
- 1/8 - teaspoon kosher salt
- ½ - cup fresh basil leaves
- 1 - tablespoon extra-virgin olive oil
- 1 - tablespoon balsamic vinegar
- ½ - teaspoon black pepper
- ¼ - teaspoon kosher salt
- 1 - ounce diced fresh mozzarella cheese (about 1/3 cup)

Directions:

1. Join tomatoes and 1/8 tsp. legitimate salt in an enormous bowl. Let represent 5mins. Include basil leaves, olive oil, balsamic vinegar, pepper, 1/4 tsp. fit salt, and mozzarella; toss.

Nutrition: Calories 80 Fat 5.8g Protein 2g Carb 5g Sugars 4g

Watermelon-Cucumber Salad

Preparation Time: 12 Minutes
Cooking Time: 0 Minutes
Servings: 4
Ingredients:

- 1 - tablespoon olive oil
- 2 - teaspoons fresh lemon juice
- ¼ - teaspoon salt
- 2 - cups cubed seedless watermelon
- 1 - cup thinly sliced English cucumber
- ¼ - cup thinly vertically sliced red onion
- 1 - tablespoon thinly sliced fresh basil

Directions:

1. Consolidate oil, squeeze, and salt in a huge bowl, mixing great. Include watermelon, cucumber, and onion; toss well to coat. Sprinkle plate of mixed greens equally with basil.

Nutrition: Calories 60 Fat 3.5g Protein 0.8g Carb 7.6g

SNACKS

Corn Salsa

Preparation Time: 10 Minutes
Cooking Time: 15 Minutes
Servings: 4

Ingredients:

- 4 Ears Corn, large with the husk on
- 4 Tomatoes (Roma) diced and seeded
- 1 tsp. of Onion powder
- 1 tsp. of Garlic powder
- 1 Onion, diced
- ½ cup chopped Cilantro
- Black pepper and salt to taste
- 1 lime, the juice
- 1 grille jalapeno, diced

Directions:

1. Preheat the grill to 450F.
2. Place the ears corn on the grate and cook until charred. Remove husk. Cut into kernels.
3. Combine all ingredients, plus the corn and mix well. Refrigerate before serving.
4. Enjoy!

Nutrition: Calories: 120 Protein: 2f Carbs: 4g Fat: 1g

Nut Mix on the Grill

Preparation Time: 15 Minutes
Cooking Time: 20 Minutes
Servings: 8

Ingredients:

- 3 cups Mixed Nuts, salted
- 1 tsp. Thyme, dried
- 1 ½ tbsp. brown sugar, packed
- 1 tbsp. Olive oil
- ¼ tsp. of Mustard powder
- ¼ tsp. Cayenne pepper

Directions:

1. Preheat the grill to 250F with closed lid.
2. In a bowl combine the ingredients and place the nuts on a baking tray lined with parchment paper. Place the try on the grill. Cook 20 minutes.
3. Serve and enjoy!

Nutrition: Calories: 65 Protein: 23g Carbs 4g: Fat: 52g

DESSERT RECIPE

Grilled Pineapple with Chocolate Sauce

Preparation Time: 10 Minutes
Cooking Time: 25 Minutes
Servings: 8
Ingredients:

- 1 pineapple
- 8 oz bittersweet chocolate chips
- 1/2 cup spiced rum
- 1/2 cup whipping cream
- 2 tbsp light brown sugar

Directions:

1. Preheat pellet grill to 400°F.
2. De-skin, the pineapple, then slice the pineapple into 1 in cubes.
3. In a saucepan, combine chocolate chips. When chips begin to melt, add rum to the saucepan. Continue to stir until combined, then add a splash of the pineapple's juice.
4. Add in whipping cream and continue to stir the mixture. Once the sauce is smooth and thickening, lower heat to simmer to keep warm.
5. Thread pineapple cubes onto skewers. Sprinkle skewers with brown sugar.
6. Place skewers on the grill grate. Grill for about 5 minutes per side, or until grill marks begin to develop.
7. Remove skewers from grill and allow to rest on a plate for about 5 minutes. Serve alongside warm chocolate sauce for dipping.

Nutrition: Calories: 112.6 Fat: 0.5 g Cholesterol: 0 Carbohydrate: 28.8 g Fiber: 1.6 g Sugar: 0.1 g Protein: 0.4 g

Nectarine and Nutella Sundae

Preparation Time: 10 Minutes
Cooking Time: 25 Minutes
Servings: 4
Ingredients:

- 2nectarines halved and pitted
- 2tsp honey
- 4tbsp Nutella
- 4scoops vanilla ice cream
- 1/4 cup pecans, chopped
- Whipped cream, to top
- 4cherries, to top

Directions:

1. Preheat pellet grill to 400°F.
2. Slice nectarines in half and remove the pits.
3. Brush the inside (cut side) of each nectarine half with honey.
4. Place nectarines directly on the grill grate, cut side down—Cook for 5-6 minutes, or until grill marks develop.
5. Flip nectarines and cook on the other side for about 2 minutes.
6. Remove nectarines from the grill and allow it to cool.
7. Fill the pit cavity on each nectarine half with 1 tbsp Nutella.
8. Place one scoop of ice cream on top of Nutella. Top with whipped cream, cherries, and sprinkle chopped pecans. Serve and enjoy!

Nutrition: Calories: 90 Fat: 3 g Carbohydrate: 15g Sugar: 13 g Protein: 2 g

Cinnamon Sugar Donut Holes

Preparation Time: 10 Minutes
Cooking Time: 35 Minutes
Servings: 4
Ingredients:

- 1/2 cup flour
- 1 tbsp cornstarch
- 1/2 tsp baking powder
- 1/8 tsp baking soda
- 1/8 tsp ground cinnamon
- 1/2 tsp kosher salt
- 1/4 cup buttermilk
- 1/4 cup sugar
- 1 1/2 tbsp butter, melted
- 1 egg
- 1/2 tsp vanilla
- Topping
- 2 tbsp sugar
- 1 tbsp sugar
- 1 tsp ground cinnamon

Directions:

1. Preheat pellet grill to 350°F.
2. In a medium bowl, combine flour, cornstarch, baking powder, baking soda, ground cinnamon, and kosher salt. Whisk to combine.
3. In a separate bowl, combine buttermilk, sugar, melted butter, egg, and vanilla. Whisk until the egg is thoroughly combined.
4. Pour wet mixture into the flour mixture and stir. Stir just until combined, careful not to overwork the mixture.
5. Spray mini muffin tin with cooking spray.
6. Spoon 1 tbsp of donut mixture into each mini muffin hole.
7. Place the tin on the pellet grill grate and bake for about 18 minutes, or until a toothpick can come out clean.
8. Remove muffin tin from the grill and let rest for about 5 minutes.
9. In a small bowl, combine 1 tbsp sugar and 1 tsp ground cinnamon.
10. Melt 2 tbsp of butter in a glass dish. Dip each donut hole in the melted butter, then mix and toss with cinnamon sugar. Place completed donut holes on a plate to serve.

Nutrition: Calories: 190 Fat: 17 g Carbohydrate: 21 g Fiber: 1 g Sugar: 8 g Protein: 3 g

SAUCES AND RUBS

Heavenly Rabbit Smoke

Preparation Time: 10 minutes
Cooking Time: Nil
Serving: 5
Ingredients
- 1 teaspoon dried thyme
- 1 teaspoon dried parsley
- 2 teaspoons dried oregano
- ½ teaspoon dried marjoram
- ½ teaspoon ground nutmeg
- ½ teaspoon ground cinnamon
- 1 teaspoon chicken bouillon granules
- 1 and ½ teaspoons garlic powder
- 1 teaspoon cracked pepper
- ½ teaspoon salt
- 1 and ½ teaspoon onion powder

Directions:

1. Mix the ingredients mentioned above to prepare the seasoning and use it as needed.

Nutrition: Calories: 20 Carbs: 5g Protein: 1g

Uncle Johnny's Rub

Preparation Time: 10 minutes
Cooking Time: Nil
Serving: 4
Ingredients
- ½ teaspoon oregano
- 4 tablespoons ground paprika
- 1 tablespoon brown sugar
- 1 tablespoon ground cumin
- 1 tablespoon chili powder
- 1 tablespoon mustard powder
- 1 tablespoon salt
- 2 tablespoons pepper
- 1 tablespoon garlic powder

Directions:

1. Mix the ingredients mentioned above to prepare the seasoning and use it as needed.

Nutrition: Calories: 20 Carbs: 5g Protein: 1g

Fajita Seasoning
Preparation Time: 10 minutes
Cooking Time: Nil
Serving: 4
Ingredients
- ¼ cup of chili powder
- 2 tablespoon of ground cumin
- 1 tablespoon of salt
- 4 teaspoons of black pepper
- 3 teaspoons of dried oregano
- 2 teaspoons of paprika
- 1 teaspoon of onion powder
- 1 teaspoon of parsley

Directions:

1. Mix the ingredients mentioned above to prepare the seasoning and use it as needed.

Nutrition: Calories: 20 Carbs: 5g Protein: 1g

NUT AND FRUIT RECIPES

Smoked Bananas Foster Bread Pudding

Preparation Time: 1 hour

Cooking Time: 2 hours 15 minutes

Servings: 8 to 10

Ingredients:

- 1loaf (about 4 cups) brioche or challah, cubed into 1-inch cubes
- 3eggs, lightly beaten
- 2cups of milk
- 2/3 cups sugar
- 2large bananas, peeled and smashed
- 1tbsp vanilla extract
- 1tbsp cinnamon
- 1/4 tsp. nutmeg
- 1/2 cup pecans
- Rum Sauce Ingredients:
- 1/2 cup spiced rum
- 1/4 cup unsalted butter
- 1cup dark brown sugar
- 1tsp cinnamon
- 5large bananas, peeled and quartered

Directions:

1. Place pecans on a skillet over medium heat and lightly toast for about 5 minutes, until you can smell them.
2. Remove from heat and allow cooling. Once cooled, chop pecans.
3. Lightly butter a 9" x 13" baking dish and evenly layer bread cubes in the container.
4. In a large bowl, whisk eggs, milk, sugar, mashed bananas, vanilla extract, cinnamon, and nutmeg.
5. Whip the egg mixture over the bread in the baking dish evenly. Sprinkle with chopped pecans. Cover with aluminum foil and refrigerate for about 30 minutes.
6. Preheat pellet grill to 180degrees F. Turn your smoke setting to high, if applicable.
7. Remove foil from dish and place on the smoker for 5 minutes with the lid closed, allowing bread to absorb smoky flavor.
8. Remove the dish from the grill and cover with foil again. Increase your pellet grill's temperature to 350degrees F.
9. Place dish on the grill grate and cook for 50-60 minutes until everything is cooked through and the bread pudding is bubbling.
10. In a saucepan, while pudding cooks, heat butter for rum sauce over medium heat. If the butter begins to melt, add the brown sugar, cinnamon, and bananas. Sauté until bananas start to soften.

11. Add rum and watch. When the liquid begins to bubble, light a match, and tilt the pan. Slowly and carefully move the game towards the fluid until the sauce lights. When the flames go away, remove the skillet from heat.
12. If you're uncomfortable lighting the liquid with a match, just cook it for 3-4 minutes over medium heat after the rum has been added.
13. Keep rum sauce on a simmer or reheat once it's time to serve.
14. Remove bread pudding from the grill and allow it to cool for about 5 minutes.
15. Cut into squares, put each square on a plate, add a banana piece, and then drizzle rum sauce over the top. Serve on its own or a la mode and enjoy it!

Nutrition: Calories: 274.7 Fat: 7.9 g Cholesterol: 10 mg Carbohydrate: 35.5 g Fiber: 0.9 g Sugar: 24.7 g Protein: 4 g

TRADITIONAL RECIPES

Sweet & Spicy Chicken Thighs

Preparation Time: 15 minutes
Cooking Time: 15 minutes
Servings: 4
Ingredients:

- 2 garlic cloves, minced
- ¼ cup honey
- 2 tablespoons soy sauce
- ¼ teaspoon red pepper flakes, crushed
- 4 (5-ounce) skinless, boneless chicken thighs
- 2 tablespoons olive oil
- 2 teaspoons sweet rub
- ¼ teaspoon red chili powder
- Ground black pepper, as required

Directions

1. Preheat the Blackstone grill & Smoker on grill setting to 400 degrees F.
2. In a small bowl, add garlic, honey, soy sauce and red pepper flakes and with a wire whisk, beat until well combined.
3. Coat chicken thighs with oil and season with sweet rub, chili powder and black pepper generously.
4. Arrange the chicken drumsticks onto the grill and cook for about 15 minutes per
5. In the last 4-5 minutes of cooking, coat drumsticks with garlic mixture.
6. Serve immediately.

Nutrition: Calories 309 Total Fat 12.1 g Saturated Fat 2.9 g Cholesterol 82 mg Sodium 504 mg Total Carbs 18.7 g Fiber 0.2 g Sugar 17.6 g Protein 32.3 g

SAUCES, RUBS, AND MARINATES

Classic Kansas City BBQ Sauce

Preparation Time: 10 Minutes
Cooking Time: 15 Minutes
Servings: 24
Ingredients:

- 1/4 cup yellow onion, finely chopped
- 2 tablespoons water
- 2 tablespoons vegetable oil
- 2 cups ketchup
- 1/3 cup brown sugar
- 3 cloves garlic, finely chopped
- 1 tablespoon apple cider vinegar
- 1 tablespoon tomato paste
- 1 tablespoon Worcestershire sauce
- 1 teaspoon liquid hickory smoke
- 1 teaspoon ground mustard

Directions:

1. Place the onion in a food processor and pulse until pureed. Add the water to the onion and pulse few more times.
2. In a medium saucepan, heat the oil and add the onion. When the onion is just starting to soften, add the remaining ingredients and stir well.
3. Stretch or roll dough to a 12-inch circle.
4. Cook the sauce at a simmer for fifteen minutes, stirring occasionally.
5. Remove the pan from the heat and allow to cool for thirty minutes before using or storing in a mason jar.

Nutrition: Calories: 799 Sodium: 595mg Dietary Fiber: 8.6g Fat: 52.7g Carbs: 74.9g Protein: 10g

RUBS, INJECTABLES, MARINADES, AND MOPS

Not-Just-For-Pork Rub
Preparation Time: 10 Minutes
Cooking Time: 0 Minutes
Servings: ¼ Cup
Ingredients:
- ½ teaspoon ground thyme
- ½ teaspoon paprika
- ½ teaspoon course kosher salt
- ½ teaspoon garlic powder
- ½ teaspoon onion powder
- ½ teaspoon chili powder
- ¼ teaspoon dried oregano leaves
- ¼ teaspoon freshly ground black pepper
- ¼ teaspoon ground chipotle chile pepper
- ¼ teaspoon celery seed

Directions:
1. In a small airtight container or zip-top bag, combine the thyme, paprika, salt, garlic powder, onion powder, chili powder, oregano, black pepper, chipotle pepper, and celery seed. Close the container and shake to mix. Unused rub will keep in an airtight container for months.

Nutrition: Calories: 20 Carbs: 5g Protein: 1g

Chicken Rub

Preparation Time: 10 Minutes
Cooking Time: 0 Minutes
Servings: ¼ Cup
Ingredients:
- 2 tablespoons packed light brown sugar
- 1½ teaspoons course kosher salt
- 1¼ teaspoons garlic powder
- ½ teaspoon onion powder
- ½ teaspoon freshly ground black pepper
- ½ teaspoon ground chipotle chile pepper
- ½ teaspoon smoked paprika
- ¼ teaspoon dried oregano leaves
- ¼ teaspoon mustard powder
- ¼ teaspoon cayenne pepper

Directions:

1. In a small airtight container or zip-top bag, combine the brown sugar, salt, garlic powder, onion powder, black pepper, chipotle pepper, paprika, oregano, mustard, and cayenne. Close the container and shake to mix. Unused rub will keep in an airtight container for months.

Nutrition: Calories: 20 Carbs: 5g Protein: 1g

OTHER RECIPES YOU NEVER THOUGHT ABOUT TO GRILL

Summer Treat Corn

Preparation time: 10 minutes
Cooking time 20 minutes
Servings: 6
Ingredients

- 6 fresh whole corn on the cob
- One-half C. butter
- Salt

Direction
1. Set the temperature of Blackstone Grill to 400 degrees F and preheat with closed lid for 15 mins.
2. Husk the corn and remove all the silk.
3. Brush each corn with melted butter and sprinkle with salt.
4. Place the corn onto the grill and cook for about 20 mins, rotating after every 5 mins and brushing with butter once halfway through.
5. Serve warm.

Nutrition: Energy (calories): 1196 kcal Protein: 30.76 g Fat: 38.84 g Carbohydrates: 218.81 g Calcium, Ca35 mg Magnesium, Mg280 mg Phosphorus, P745 mg Iron, Fe6 mg

Crunchy Potato Wedges

Preparation time: 15 minutes
Cooking time 16minutes
Servings: 5
Ingredients

- 4 Yukon gold potatoes
- 2 tbsp. olive oil
- 1 tbsp. garlic, minced
- 2 tsp. onion powder
- One-half tsp. red pepper flakes, crushed
- Salt and freshly ground black pepper, to taste

Direction

1. Keep the oven of the Blackstone Grill to 400 degrees F and heat it up it for 15 minuteswith the cover closed.
2. Cut each potato into 8 equal-sized wedges.
3. In a large bowl, add potato wedges and remaining ingredients and toss to coat well.
4. Arrange the potato wedges onto the grill and cook for about 8 mins per side.
5. Remove from grill and serve hot.

Nutrition: Energy (calories): 353 kcal Protein: 7.83 g Fat: 7.12 g Carbohydrates: 66.65 g Calcium, Ca54 mg Magnesium, Mg88 mg Phosphorus, P220 m Iron, Fe3.07 mg

Twice Grilled Potatoes

Preparation time: 20 minutes
Cooking time 4 hours
Servings: 4
Ingredients

- 6 russet potatoes
- 2 tbsp. olive oil
- Salt
- 8 cooked bacon slices, crumbled
- One-half C. heavy whipping cream
- 4 oz. cream cheese, softened
- 4 tbsp. butter, softened
- 1 tsp. seasoned salt
- 2 C. Monterrey Jack cheese, grated and divided

Direction

1. Preheat oven to 500 degrees.
2. Cut potatoes into thin wedges and transfer to a large bowl.
3. Add 1 Tbsp. oil, and salt, to bowl. Toss to coat.
4. Separate potatoes into 2 even piles on baking sheet.
5. Bake 4 hours, turning once. Remove from oven and let cool.
6. Turn oven to broil. Combine cream, butter, and 2 tbsp. of cheese.
7. Place potatoes into 2 10-oz. or 1 6-oz. oven-save bowl.
8. Top with half of the cheese, then half of the cream mixture.
9. Repeat layers. Broil until cream cheese is bubbly and golden.
10. Top with remaining 2 tbsp. olive oil and seasoned salt.
11. Serve.

Nutrition: Energy (calories): 1192 kcal Protein: 36.96 g Fat: 72.77 g Carbohydrates: 102.32 g Calcium, Ca600 mg Magnesium, Mg154 mgPhosphorus, P730 mg Iron, Fe5.82 mg

Mouthwatering Cauliflower

Preparation time: 15 minutes
Cooking time 30 minutes
Servings: 8
Ingredients

- 2 large heads cauliflower head, stem removed and cut into 2-inch florets
- 3 tbsp. olive oil
- Salt
- ground black pepper
- One-fourth C parsley, chopped finely

Direction

1. Control the frequency of the grill to 500 degrees F and set the temperature this for 15 minutes with the lid close.
2. Add cauliflower florets, oil, salt and black pepper and toss to coat well.
3. Divide the cauliflower florets onto 2 baking sheets and spread in an even layer.
4. Place the baking sheets onto the grill and cook for about 20-30 mins, stirring once after 15 mins.
5. Transfer into a large bowl.
6. Add the parsley and toss to coat well.
7. Serve.

Nutrition: Energy (calories): 65 kcal Protein: 1.52 g Fat: 5.32 g Carbohydrates: 3.95 g Calcium, Ca26 mg Magnesium, Mg14 mg Phosphorus, P34 mg Iron, Fe0.8 mg Potassium, K244 mg

Super-Addicting Mushrooms

Preparation time: 15 minutes
Cooking time 45 minutes
Servings: 4
Ingredients

- 4 C. fresh whole baby Portobello mushrooms, cleaned
- 1 tbsp. canola oil
- 1 tsp. granulated garlic
- 1 tsp. onion powder
- Salt and freshly ground black pepper, to taste

Direction

1. Put a Blackstone Grill fire to 180 degrees F and pre - heat for 15 mins with the coverclosed, using charcoal.
2. Add all ingredients and mix well.
3. Place the mushrooms onto the grill and cook for about 30 mins.
4. Preheat the Grill to 400 degrees F and preheat with closed lid for 15 mins.
5. Place the mushrooms onto the grill and cook for about 15 mins.
6. Serve warm.

Nutrition: Energy (calories): 69 kcal Protein: 4.08 g Fat: 4.21 g Carbohydrates: 6.08 g Calcium, Ca7 mg Magnesium, Mg17 mg Phosphorus, P166 mg Iron, Fe0.52 mg Fiber2.8 g Sugars, total2.78 g

Veggie Lover's Burgers

Preparation time: 20 minutes
Cooking time 47 minutes
Servings: 6

Ingredients

- Three-fourth C. lentils
- 1 tbsp. ground flaxseed
- 2 tbsp. extra-virgin olive oil
- 1 onion, chopped
- 2 garlic cloves, minced
- Salt
- black pepper
- 1 C. walnuts, toasted
- Three-fourth C. breadcrumbs
- 1 tsp. ground cumin
- 1 tsp. paprika

Direction

1. Cook lentils by boiling in 2 qt. salted water for 25 minutes or till tender. Drain. Heat oil in a large nonstick skillet over medium-high heat. Add onion and cook for 5 to 7 minutes, until onion is translucent.
2. Place one-fourth cup lentils into a food processor; add 1 tbsp. flaxseed and 1 tbsp. water. Blend until smooth. Add flaxseed lentil mixture to skillet and cook for 1 minute. Add garlic, salt, and pepper; cook for 2 minutes. Mash mixture with a potato masher.
3. Combine the rest of ingredients in a food processor. Puree until the mixture forms a dough. Add one-fourth cup breadcrumb-walnut mixture to the remaining lentils in the skillet and cook for 1 to 2 minutes, until the mixture is dr.
4. Heat the smoker to 400° F. Line a baking sheet with parchment paper
5. Shape the lentil mixture into four 3-inch patties. Place patties on prepared baking sheet and bake for 45 minutes, until golden brown.
6. Put burgers on a bun with your favorite toppings.

Nutrition: Energy (calories): 157 kcal Protein: 3.95 g Fat: 11.68 g Carbohydrates: 12.07 g Calcium, Ca32 mg Magnesium, Mg39 mg Phosphorus, P93 mg Iron, Fe1.37 mg

Satisfying Veggie Casserole

Preparation time: 15 minutes
Cooking time 50 minutes
Servings: 10
Ingredients

- 5 tbsp. olive oil, divided
- 6 C. onions, sliced thinly
- 1 tbsp. fresh thyme, chopped and divided
- Salt and freshly ground black pepper, to taste
- 1 tbsp. unsalted butter
- 1 and one-fourth lb. Yukon gold potatoes, peeled and 1/8-inch thick slices
- One-half. heavy cream
- 2 and one-fourth lb. tomatoes, cut into one-fourth-inch thick slices
- One-fourth cup black olives, pitted and sliced

Direction

1. Heat 3 tablespoons of the olive oil over a medium-high flame. Cook onions, stirring occasionally until they turn translucent. Sprinkle thyme and add salt and pepper to taste. Continue cooking for 5 to 10 minutes over a medium heat. Stir occasionally.
2. Heat a grill to medium-high. Brush potatoes with the remaining olive oil and arrange in a single layer on the grill. Cook for 8 to 10 minutes, until lightly browned, turning once. Cut into half- inch thick slices.
3. Preheat oven to 375°F. Sprinkle olives on top. Pour the heavy cream over tomatoes. Cover and bake in the oven for 30 minutes or until bubbly and golden brown.
4. Enjoy!

Nutrition: Energy (calories): 158 kcal Protein: 2.74 g Fat: 9.31 g Carbohydrates: 17.97 g Calcium, Ca45 mg Magnesium, Mg29 m Phosphorus, P80 mg Iron, Fe1.48 mg Potassium, K529 mg

North American Pot Pie

Preparation time: 15 minutes
Cooking time 50 minutes
Servings: 10

Ingredients

- 2 tbsp. cornstarch
- 2 tbsp. water
- 3 C. chicken broth
- 1 C. milk
- 3 tbsp. butter
- 1 tbsp. fresh rosemary, chopped
- 1 tbsp. fresh thyme, chopped
- Salt and freshly ground black pepper, to taste
- 2 and three-fourth C. frozen chopped broccoli, thawed
- 3 C. frozen peas, thawed
- 3 C. chopped frozen carrots, thawed
- 1 frozen puff pastry sheet

Direction

1. Heat the oven to 450, and lightly grease a mug or small baking dish.
2. In a large bowl, dissolve the cornstarch with the water. Stir in the broth, milk, butter, rosemary, thyme, salt and pepper.
3. Add the vegetables and stir. Add the filling to the cooking dish.
4. Lay the puff pastry over the filling, and tuck the sides into the dish so that the pastry overlaps.
5. Bake for 50 minutes, or until the pastry is brown. Serve hot.

Nutrition: Energy (calories): 76 kcal Protein: 2.55 g Fat: 4.28 g Carbohydrates: 7.79 g Calcium, Ca64 mg Magnesium, Mg14 mg Phosphorus, P55 mg Iron, Fe0.49 mg Cholesterol13 mg

Potluck Favorite Baked Beans

Preparation time: 15 minutes
Cooking time 2-3 hours
Servings: 10
Ingredients

- 1 tbsp. butter
- One-half of red bell pepper
- One-half of medium onion, chopped
- 2 jalapeño peppers, chopped
- 2 (28-oz.) cans baked beans, rinsed and drained
- 8 oz. pineapple chunks, drained
- 1 C. BBQ sauce
- 1 C. brown sugar
- 1 tbsp. ground mustard

Direction

1. Prepare your Smoker and heat it for 450F.
2. Melt butter over medium heat and sauté the spices for about 4-5 mins.
3. Transfer the pepper mixture into a bowl.
4. Add remaining ingredients and stir to combine.
5. Transfer the mixture into a Dutch oven.
6. Place the Dutch oven onto the grill and cook for about 2-3 hours.
7. Serve hot.

Nutrition: Energy (calories): 86 kcal Protein: 0.97 g Fat: 1.48 g Carbohydrates: 18.57 g Calcium, Ca16 mg Magnesium, Mg12 mg Phosphorus, P22 mg Iron, Fe0.42 mg Fiber1.1 g

Traditional English Mac n' Cheese

Preparation time: 15 minutes
Cooking time 30 minutes
Servings: 10

Ingredients

- 2 lb. elbow macaroni
- Three-fourth C. butter
- One-half C. flour
- 1 tsp. dry mustard
- 1 and one-half C. milk
- 2 lb. Velveeta cheese,
- Salt
- black pepper
- 1 and one-half C. cheddar cheese, shredded
- 2 C. plain dry breadcrumbs
- Paprika

Direction

1. Cook macaroni for 8-10 minutes under directed time in boiling water. Reserve 1/3 C. of macaroni water. In separate sauce pan, melt butter. Stir in flour and mustard until smooth.
2. Add milk and cook over medium heat, stirring constantly, until thickened and bubbly. Stir in cheese and macaroni water. Season with salt and pepper. Add cooked macaroni to saucepan and stir to coat with sauce. Garnish with the extra cheddar cheese and dust with the bread crumbs and paprika. Place in a smoky grill in a 300-degree Fahrenheit oven for 20 minutes or until golden brown. Serve immediately.

Nutrition: Energy (calories): 951 kcal Protein: 41.91 g Fat: 35.95 g Carbohydrates: 113.49 g Calcium, Ca998 mg Magnesium, Mg77 mg Phosphorus, P1850 mg Iron, Fe2.94 mg

Amazing Irish Soda Bread

Preparation time: 15 minutes
Cooking time 1 hour and 15 minutes
Servings: 10

Ingredients

- 4 C. flour
- 1 C. raisins
- One-half C. sugar
- 1 tbsp. caraway seeds
- 2 tsp. baking powder
- 1 tsp. baking soda
- Three-fourth tsp. salt
- 1 and one-fourth C. buttermilk
- 1 C. sour cream
- 2 eggs

Direction

1. Preheat the Blackstone grill to 375 degrees F. Mix the dry ingredients together in a large bowl. Be sure to measure and combine well.
2. Add the sour cream, eggs, and buttermilk into the dry ingredients. Mix until all of the ingredients are wet. Remove the dough from the bowl and form it into a rectangular loaf.
3. Bake for 60 minutes at 375 F. After 45 minutes, remove the baking sheet from the oven and spread what remaining dough there is into a wider loaf. Return to the oven for the last 15 minutes or so.
4. Allow to cool for 30 minutes. Serve.

Nutrition: Energy (calories): 286 kcal Protein: 9.71 g Fat: 6.25 Carbohydrates: 47.1 g Calcium, Ca132 mg Magnesium, Mg21 mg Phosphorus, P197 mg Iron, Fe3.08 mg Potassium, K288 mg;

Native Southern Cornbread

Preparation time: 15 minutes
Cooking time 30 minutes
Servings: 8
Ingredients

- 2 tbsp. butter
- 1 and one-half C. all-purpose flour
- 1 and one-half C. yellow cornmeal
- 2 tbsp. sugar
- 3 tsp. baking powder
- Three-fourth tsp. baking soda
- Three-fourth tsp. salt
- 1 C. whole milk
- 1 C. buttermilk
- 3 large eggs
- 3 tbsp. butter, melted

Direction

1. Sift together the dry ingredients. Then add the wet ingredients. Stir just until moistened, but do not overbeat.
2. Put a 3-quart cast iron skillet in the preheated oven and heat oven to 375 degrees. Pour the batter into the hot skillet and return the skillet to the oven. Bake cornbread for 25 to 30 min. until the top is golden brown. Remove cornbread from the oven and let it sit for 10 min. before serving.

Nutrition: Energy (calories): 259 kcal Protein: 6.42 g Fat: 11 g Carbohydrates: 33.67 g Calcium, Ca176 mg Magnesium, Mg18 mg Phosphorus, P246 mg Iron, Fe1.31 mg Fiber1.2 g

CONCLUSION

In conclusion, it is a fact that the Blackstone pellet grill has made grilling easier and better for humanity, and Grilling, which is part of the so-called "dietetic" cooking, had been made easier through the Blackstone grill. Giving us that tasty meal, we've been craving for and thus improving the quality of life. This book made you a lot of recipes that you can make at your home with your new Blackstone Pellet grill. The recipes will give so much satisfaction with the tenderness and tasty BBQ.

The Blackstone barbecues are electrical, and a typical 3-position function controls them. A cylindrical device transmits the pellets from the storage to the fire place, like a pellet stove. Blackstone Grill smoker promotes an excellent outcome for your meat and other recipes. This smoker provides a tasty for your foods. To achieve such a real taste, you need the quality of materials and get the exact smoking. It is best if you get the maximum consistency of smoking so that you can have the best result of your meat and other recipes. Moreover, if you add more flavors to your recipes, use the best wood pellet for cooking for your food.

Many people ask me questions on why I chose Blackstone pellet grill, and you might think, well, the answer is clear and true, and yes! It's right before us. Why?

It cooks with a wood fire, giving an excellent quality in taste because nothing is like it: real wood, real smoking, natural aroma. In terms of the cooking process, it has changed a lot. Experts chefs tend to have new experiments with new flavor and ingredients to create a delicious and tasty recipe.

Grilling is one of the most popular cooking processes that grant a perfect taste to your recipes. Grilling is a much healthier method than others because its benefits food, preserves flavor, and nutrients. But from the other side, a Blackstone grill smoker's wood pellet grill allows you

to grill your food quickly and with less effort and smoke. The advantage of having a Blackstone grill smoker in your home is the versatility, helps you cook food faster, provides a monitoring scale for the temperature, and it is one of the essential parts of cooking.

It is a versatile barbecue. In fact, it can be grilled, smoked, baked, roasted, and stewed—everything you can imagine cooking with the Blackstone grill smoker. You will find that this Blackstone grill smoker is aflexible tool that has a good service.

As we all could testify that using the pellet grill has been made simple by Blackstone: its intuitive control panel has a power button and a knobthat allows you to adjust the temperature comfortably.

Finally, we need to note that through Grilling, we can always find new flavors in our dishes: with Blackstone pellets, you can smoke your dishes, giving them an ever new and different flavor. Blackstone Grill smoker isthe answer you are looking for your taste buds. Don't waste your time and have your own smoker at home and start cooking your favorite recipes with this book.

BLACKSTONE OUTDOOR GAS GRIDDLE COOKBOOK FOR BEGINNERS:

100 of the Most Amazing Beef, Pork and Lamb Recipes, Discover how to EnhanceFlavor with Grilling

Mark Franklin

GRILL BEEF RECIPES

BBQ Spiced Flank Steak

Preparation Time: 15 minutes
Cooking Time: 30 minutes
Servings: 6
Ingredients:

- 1 (2-pound) beef flank steak
- 2 tablespoons olive oil
- ¼ cup BBQ rub
- 3 tablespoons blue cheese, crumbled
- 2 tablespoons butter, softened
- 1 teaspoon fresh chives, minced

Directions:

1. Preheat the Z Grills Blackstone Grill & Smoker on grill setting to 225 degrees F.
2. Coat the steak with oil evenly and season with BBQ rub.
3. Place the steak onto the grill and cook for about 10-15 minutes per side.
4. Remove the steak from grill and place onto a cutting board for about 10 minutes before slicing.
5. Meanwhile, in a bowl, add blue cheese, butter and chives and mix well.
6. With a sharp knife, cut the steak into thin strips across the grain.
7. Top with cheese mixture and serve.

Nutrition: Calories 370 Total Fat 19.1 g Saturated Fat 7.5 g Cholesterol 148 mg Sodium 1666 mg Total Carbs 0.1 g Fiber 0 g Sugar 0 g Protein 46.8 g

Beef Stuffed Bell Peppers

Preparation Time: 20 minutes
Cooking Time: 1 hour
Servings: 6
Ingredients:

- 6 large bell peppers
- 1 pound ground beef
- 1 small onion, chopped
- 2 garlic cloves, minced
- 2 cups cooked rice
- 1 cup frozen corn, thawed
- 1 cup cooked black beans
- 2/3 cup salsa
- 2 tablespoons Cajun rub
- 1½ cups Monterey Jack cheese, grated

Directions:

1. Cut each bell pepper in half lengthwise through the stem.
2. Carefully, remove the seeds and ribs.
3. For stuffing: heat a large frying pan and cook the beef for about 6-7 minutes or until browned completely.
4. Add onion and garlic and cook for about 2-3 minutes.
5. Stir in remaining ingredients except cheese and cook for about 5 minutes.
6. Remove from the heat and set aside to cool slightly.
7. Preheat the Z Grills Blackstone Grill & Smoker on grill setting to 350 degrees F.
8. Stuff each bell pepper half with stuffing mixture evenly.
9. Arrange the peppers onto grill, stuffing side up and cook for about 40 minutes.
10. Sprinkle each bell pepper half with cheese and cook for about 5 minutes more.
11. Remove the bell peppers from grill and serve hot.

Nutrition: Calories 675 Total Fat 14.8 g Saturated Fat 7.5 g Cholesterol 93 mg Sodium 1167 mg Total Carbs 90.7 g Fiber 8.7 g Sugar 9.1 g Protein 43.9 g

BBQ Meatloaf

Preparation Time: 20 minutes
Cooking Time: 2½ hours
Servings: 8
Ingredients:

For Meatloaf:

- 3 pounds ground beef
- 3 eggs
- ½ cup panko breadcrumbs
- 1 (10-ounce) can diced tomatoes with green chile peppers
- 1 large white onion, chopped
- 2 hot banana peppers, chopped
- 2 tablespoons seasoned salt
- 2 teaspoons liquid smoke flavoring
- 2 teaspoons smoked paprika
- 1 teaspoons onion salt
- 1 teaspoons garlic salt
- Salt and ground black pepper, as required

For Sauce:

- ½ cup ketchup
- ¼ cup tomato-based chile sauce
- ¼ cup white sugar
- 2 teaspoons Worcestershire sauce
- 2 teaspoons hot pepper sauce
- 1 teaspoon red pepper flakes, crushed
- 1 teaspoon red chili pepper
- Salt and ground black pepper, as required

Directions:

1. Preheat the Z Grills Blackstone Grill & Smoker on smoke setting to 225 degrees F, usingcharcoal. Grease a loaf pan.
2. For meatloaf: in a bowl, add all ingredients and with your hands, mix until well combined. Place the mixture into prepared loaf pan evenly.
3. Place the pan onto the grill and cook for about 2 hours.
4. For sauce: in a bowl, add all ingredients and beat until well combined.
5. Remove the pan from grill and drain excess grease from meatloaf.
6. Place sauce over meatloaf evenly and place the pan onto the grill.
7. Cook for about 30 minutes. Remove the meatloaf from grill and set aside for about 10 minutes before serving. Carefully, invert the meatloaf onto a platter.
8. Cut the meatloaf into desired-sized slices and serve.

Nutrition: Calories 423 Total Fat 13 g Saturated Fat 4.7 g Cholesterol 213 mg Sodium 1879 mg Total Carbs 15.7 g Fiber 1.5 g Sugar 12.3 g Protein 54.9 g

Smoked Beef Brisket in Sweet and Spicy Rub

Preparation Time: 15 minutes
Cooking Time: 1 hour
Servings: 10
Ingredients:

- Beef Brisket (6-lbs., 2.7-kgs)
- 1 cup paprika
- ½ cup salt
- 1 cup brown sugar
- ½ cup cumin
- ½ cup pepper
- ½ cup chili powder ¼ cup cayenne pepper

Directions:

1. Combine paprika, salt, brown sugar, cumin, pepper, chili powder, and cayenne pepper in a bowl then stir until incorporated.
2. Rub the beef brisket with the spice mixture then marinate overnight. Store in the refrigerator to keep it fresh.
3. Remove the beef brisket from the refrigerator then thaw until it reaches room temperature.
4. Preheat the smoker to 250°F (121°C) with charcoal and hickory chips—using indirect heat. Don't forget to soak the wood chips before using.
5. When the smoker has reached the desired temperature, wrap the beef brisket with aluminum foil then place it in the smoker.
6. Smoke the wrapped beef brisket for 8 hours. Check the temperature every hour then adds more charcoal and hickory chips if it is necessary.
7. Once the smoked beef brisket is ready, remove from the smoker then let it sit for a few minutes until warm.
8. Unwrap the smoked beef brisket then place on a flat surface.
9. Cut the smoked beef brisket into thick slices then place on a serving dish.
10. Serve and enjoy.

Nutrition: Calories: 180 Carbs: 3g Fat: 3g Protein: 35g

Simple Smoked Beef Brisket with Mocha Sauce

Preparation Time: 15 minutes
Cooking Time: 1 hour
Servings: 10
Ingredients:

- 5 pounds beef brisket
- 1 ½ tablespoons garlic powder
- 1 ½ tablespoons onion powder
- 4 tablespoons salt
- 4 tablespoons pepper
- 2 ½ tablespoons olive oil
- 1 cup chopped onion
- 2 teaspoons salt
- ¼ cup chopped chocolate dark
- ¼ cup sugar –
- ½ cup beer –
- 2 shots espresso

Directions:

1. Rub the beef brisket with garlic powder, onion powder, salt, and black pepper.
2. Wrap the seasoned beef brisket with a sheet of plastic wrap then store in the refrigerator overnight.
3. In the morning, remove the beef brisket from the refrigerator and thaw for about an hour.
4. Preheat the smoker to 250°F (121°C) with charcoal and hickory chips—using indirect heat. Place the beef brisket in the smoker and smoke for 8 hours.
5. Keep the temperature remain at 250°F (121°C) and add some more charcoal and hickory chips if it is necessary.
6. Meanwhile, preheat a saucepan over medium heat then pour olive oil into the saucepan.
7. Once the oil is hot, stir in chopped onion then sauté until wilted and aromatic.
8. Reduce the heat to low then add the remaining sauce ingredients to the saucepan. Mix well then bring to a simmer.
9. Remove the sauce from heat then set aside.
10. When the smoked beef brisket is ready, or the internal temperature has reached 190°F (88°C), remove from the smoker then transfer to a serving dish.
11. Drizzle the mocha sauce over the smoked beef brisket then serve.
12. Enjoy warm.

Nutrition: Calories: 210 Carbs: 1g Fat: 13g Protein: 19g

Lemon Ginger Smoked Beef Ribs

Preparation Time: 10 minutes
Cooking Time: 10 hours
Servings: 10
Ingredients:

- 6 pounds beef ribs
- 3 tablespoons paprika
- ¼ cup brown sugar
- 1 ½ tablespoons dry mustard
- 1 ½ tablespoons ginger
- 1 tablespoon onion powder
- 1 ½ tablespoons salt
- 1 tablespoon pepper
- 3 tablespoons lemon juice

Directions:

1. Combine paprika with brown sugar, dry mustard, onion powder, salt, and pepper then mix well.
2. Rub the beef ribs with the spice mixture then place on a sheet of aluminum foil.
3. Splash lemon juice over the beef ribs then sprinkle ginger on top.
4. Wrap the seasoned beef ribs with the aluminum foil then set aside.
5. Preheat the smoker to 250°F (121°C) with charcoal and hickory chips—don't forget to soak the wood chips before using.
6. Place the wrapped beef ribs in the smoker and smoke for 10 hours.
7. Check the temperature remain at 250°F (121°C) and add some more charcoal and hickory chips if it is necessary.
8. Once the smoked beef ribs are done, remove from the smoker.
9. Unwrap the smoked beef ribs then place on a serving dish.
10. Serve and enjoy.

Nutrition: Calories: 415 Fat: 35g Protein: 25g

Chocolate Smoked Beef Ribs

Preparation Time: 15 minutes
Cooking Time: 19 hours
Servings: 10
Ingredients:

- 6 pounds beef ribs
- 1 ¼ cups cocoa powder
- ¾ cup chili powder
- ¾ cup sugar
- ¾ cup salt
- ¼ cup black pepper
- ¼ cup cumin

Directions:

1. Place the cocoa powder in a bowl then add chili powder, sugar, salt, black pepper, and cumin in the bowl. Mix well.
2. Rub the beef ribs with the cocoa powder mixture then cover with plastic wrap.
3. Marinate the beef ribs overnight and store in the refrigerator to keep it fresh.
4. In the morning, remove the beef ribs from the refrigerator and thaw for about an hour.
5. Preheat the smoker to 250°F (121°C) with charcoal and hickory chips—using indirect heat. Place the beef ribs in the smoker and smoke for 10 hours.
6. Keep the temperature remain at 250°F (121°C) and add some more charcoal and hickory chips if it is necessary.
7. Once it is done or the internal temperature has reached 170°F (77°C), take the smoked beef ribs out from the smoker and transfer to a serving dish.
8. Serve and enjoy warm.

Nutrition: Calories: 415 Carbs: 0g Fat: 35g Protein: 25g

GRILL PORK RECIPES

Simple Wood Pellet Smoked Pork Ribs

Preparation Time: 15 Minutes
Cooking Time: 5 Hours
Servings: 7
Ingredients:

- Three rack baby back ribs
- 3/4 cup pork and poultry rub
- 3/4 cup Que BBQ Sauce

Directions:

1. Peel the membrane from the backside of the ribs and trim any fat.
2. Season the pork generously with the rub.
3. Set the wood pellet grill to 180°F and preheat for 15 minutes with the lid closed.
4. Place the pork ribs on the grill and smoke them for 5 hours.
5. Remove it from the grill and wrap them in a foil with the BBQ sauce.
6. Place back the pork and increase the temperature to 350°F—Cook for 45 more minutes.
7. Remove the pork from the grill and let it rest for 20 minutes before serving. Enjoy.

Nutrition: Calories 762 Total Fat 57g Saturated Fat 17g Total Carbs 23g Net Carbs 22.7g Protein 39g Sugar 18g Fiber 0.5g Sodium: 737mg Potassium 618mg

Roasted Pork with Balsamic Strawberry Sauce

Preparation Time: 15 Minutes
Cooking Time: 35 Minutes
Servings: 3
Ingredients:

- 2 lb. pork tenderloin
- Salt and pepper to taste
- 2 tbsp rosemary, dried
- 2 tbsp olive oil
- 12 strawberries, fresh
- 1 cup balsamic vinegar
- 4 tbsp sugar

Directions:

1. Set the wood pellet grill to 350°F and preheat for 15 minutes with a closed lid.
2. Meanwhile, rinse the pork and pat it dry—season with salt, pepper, and rosemary.
3. In an oven skillet, heat oil until smoking. Add the pork and sear on all sides until golden brown.
4. Set the skillet in the grill and cook for 20 minutes or until the meat is no longer pink and the internal temperature is 150°F.
5. Remove the pork from the grill and let rest for 10 minutes.
6. Add berries to the skillet and sear over the stovetop for a minute. Remove the strawberries from the skillet.
7. Add vinegar in the same skillet and scrape any browned bits from the skillet bottom.
8. Slice the meat and place the strawberries on top, then drizzle vinegar sauce. Enjoy.

Nutrition: Calories 244 Total Fat 9g Saturated Fat 3g Total Carbs 15g Net Carbs 13g Protein 25g Sugar 12g Fiber 2g Sodium: 159mg

Wood Pellet Grill Pork Crown Roast

Preparation Time: 5 Minutes
Cooking Time: 60 Minutes
Servings: 5
Ingredients:

- 13 ribs pork
- 1/4 cup favorite rub
- 1 cup apple juice
- 1 cup Apricot BBQ sauce

Directions:

1. Set the wood pellet temperature to 375°F to preheat for 15 minutes with the lid closed.
2. Meanwhile, season the pork with the rub, then let sit for 30 minutes.
3. Wrap the tips of each crown roast with foil to prevent the burns from turning black.
4. Place the meat on the grill grate and cook for 90 minutes. Spray apple juice every 30 minutes.
5. When the meat has reached an internal temperature of 125°F, remove the foils.
6. Spray the roast with apple juice again and let cook until the internal temperature has reached 135°F.
7. In the latter 10 minutes of cooking, baste the roast with BBQ sauce.
8. Remove from the grill and wrap with foil. Let rest for 15 minutes before serving. Enjoy.

Nutrition: Calories 240 Total fat 16g Saturated fat 6g Protein 23g Sodium: 50mg

Wet-Rubbed St. Louis Ribs

Preparation Time: 15 Minutes
Cooking Time: 4 Hours
Servings: 3
Ingredients:

- 1/2 cup brown sugar
- 1 tbsp cumin, ground
- 1 tbsp Ancho Chile powder
- 1 tbsp smoked paprika
- 1 tbsp garlic salt
- 3 tbsp balsamic vinegar
- 1 Rack St. Louis style ribs
- 2 cup apple juice

Directions:

1. Add all the ingredients except ribs in a mixing bowl and mix until well mixed. Place the rub on both sides of the ribs and let sit for 10 minutes.
2. Set the wood pellet temperature to 180°F and preheat for 15 minutes. Smoke the ribs for 2 hours.
3. Increase the temperature to 250°F and wrap the ribs and apple juice with foil or tinfoil.
4. Place back the pork and cook for an additional 2 hours.
5. Remove from the grill and let rest for 5 minutes before serving. Enjoy.

Nutrition: Calories 210 Total fat 13g Saturated fat 4g Total Carbs 0g Net Carbs 0g Protein 24g Sodium: 85mg

Cocoa Crusted Pork Tenderloin

Preparation Time: 30 Minutes
Cooking Time: 25 Minutes
Servings: 5
Ingredients:

- One pork tenderloin
- 1/2 tbsp fennel, ground
- 2 tbsp cocoa powder, unsweetened
- 1 tbsp smoked paprika
- 1/2 tbsp kosher salt
- 1/2 tbsp black pepper
- 1 tbsp extra virgin olive oil
- Three green onion

Directions:

1. Remove the silver skin and the connective tissues from the pork loin.
2. Combine the rest of the ingredients in a mixing bowl, then rub the mixture on the pork. Refrigerate for 30 minutes.
3. Preheat the wood pellet grill for 15 minutes with the lid closed.
4. Sear all sides of the loin at the front of the grill, then reduce the temperature to 350°F **and move the pork to the center grill.**
5. Cook for 15 more minutes or until the internal temperature is 145°F.
6. Remove from grill and let rest for 10 minutes before slicing. Enjoy

Nutrition: Calories 264 Total fat 13.1g Saturated fat 6g Total Carbs 4.6g Net Carbs 1.2g Protein 33g Sugar 0g Fiber 3.4g Sodium: 66mg

Wood Pellet Grilled Bacon

Preparation Time: 30 Minutes
Cooking Time: 25 Minutes
Servings: 6
Ingredients:

- 1 lb. bacon, thickly cut

Directions:

1. Preheat your wood pellet grill to 375°F.
2. Line a baking sheet with parchment paper, then place the bacon on it in a single layer.
3. Close the lid and bake for 20 minutes. Flip over, close the top, and bake for an additional 5 minutes.
4. Serve with the favorite side and enjoy it.

Nutrition: Calories 315 Total fat 14g Saturated fat 10g Protein 9g Sodium: 500mg

Wood Pellet Grilled Pork Chops

Preparation Time: 20 Minutes
Cooking Time: 10 Minutes
Servings: 6
Ingredients:

- Six pork chops, thickly cut
- BBQ rub

Directions:

1. Preheat the wood pellet to 450°**F.**
2. Season the pork chops generously with the BBQ rub. Place the pork chops on the grill and cook for 6 minutes or until the internal temperature reaches 145°F.
3. Remove from the grill and let sit for 10 minutes before serving.
4. Enjoy.

Nutrition: Calories 264 Total fat 13g Saturated fat 6g Total Carbs 4g Net Carbs 1g Protein 33g Fiber 3g Sodium: 66mg

Wood Pellet Blackened Pork Chops

Preparation Time: 5 Minutes
Cooking Time: 20 Minutes
Servings: 6
Ingredients:

- Six pork chops
- 1/4 cup blackening seasoning
- Salt and pepper to taste

Directions:

1. Preheat your grill to 375°F.
2. Meanwhile, generously season the pork chops with the blackening seasoning, salt, and pepper.
3. Place the pork chops on the grill and close the lid.
4. Let grill for 8 minutes, then flip the chops. Cook until the internal temperature reaches 142°F.
5. Remove the chops from the grill and let rest for 10 minutes before slicing.
6. Serve and enjoy.

Nutrition: Calories 333 Total fat 18g Saturated fat 6g Total Carbs 1g Protein 40g, Fiber 1g Sodium: 3175mg

Teriyaki Pineapple Pork Tenderloin Sliders

Preparation Time: 20 Minutes
Cooking Time: 20 Minutes
Servings: 6
Ingredients:

- 1-1/2 lb. pork tenderloin
- One can pineapple ring
- One package king's Hawaiian rolls
- 8 oz teriyaki sauce
- 1-1/2 tbsp salt
- 1 tbsp onion powder
- 1 tbsp paprika
- 1/2 tbsp garlic powder
- 1/2 tbsp cayenne pepper

Directions:

1. Add all the fixings for the rub in a mixing bowl and mix until well mixed. Generously rub the pork loin with the mixture.
2. Heat the pellet to 325°F. Place the meat on a grill and cook while you turn it every 4 minutes.
3. Cook until the internal temperature reaches 145°F. remove from the grill and let it rest for 5 minutes.
4. Meanwhile, open the pineapple can and place the pineapple rings on the grill. Flip the rings when they have a dark brown color.
5. At the same time, half the rolls and place them on the grill and grill them until toasty browned.
6. Assemble the slider by putting the bottom roll first, followed by the pork tenderloin, pineapple ring, a drizzle of sauce, and top with the other roll half. Serve and enjoy.

Nutrition: Calories 243 Total fat 5g Saturated fat 2g Total Carbs 4g Net Carbs 15g Protein 33g Sugar 10g, Fiber 1g Sodium: 2447mg

Wood Pellet Grilled Tenderloin with Fresh Herb Sauce

Preparation Time: 10 Minutes
Cooking Time: 15 Minutes
Servings: 4
Ingredients:

- One pork tenderloin, silver skin removed and dried
- BBQ seasoning
- One handful basil, fresh
- 1/4 tbsp garlic powder
- 1/3 cup olive oil
- 1/2 tbsp kosher salt

Directions:

1. Preheat the wood pellet grill to medium heat.
2. Coat the pork with BBQ seasoning, then cook on semi-direct heat of the grill. Turn the pork regularly to ensure even cooking.
3. Cook until the internal temperature is 145°F. Remove from the grill and let it rest for 10 minutes.
4. Meanwhile, make the herb sauce by pulsing all the sauce ingredients in a food processor—pulse for a few times or until well chopped.
5. Slice the pork diagonally and spoon the sauce on top. Serve and enjoy.

Nutrition: Calories 300 Total fat 22g Saturated fat 4g Total Carbs 13g Net Carbs 12g Protein 14g Sugar 10g Fiber 1g Sodium: 791mg

Wood Pellet Grilled Shredded Pork Tacos

Preparation Time: 15 Minutes
Cooking Time: 7 Hours
Servings: 8
Ingredients:

- 5 lb. pork shoulder, bone-in
- 3 tbsp brown sugar
- 1 tbsp salt
- 1 tbsp garlic powder
- 1 tbsp paprika
- 1 tbsp onion powder
- 1/4 tbsp cumin
- 1 tbsp cayenne pepper

Directions:

1. Mix all the dry rub ingredients and rub on the pork shoulder.
2. Preheat the grill to 275°F and cook the pork directly for 6 hours or until the internal temperature has reached 145°F.
3. If you want to fall off the bone tender pork, then cook until the internal temperature is 190°F.
4. Let rest for 10 minutes before serving. Enjoy

Nutrition: Calories 566 Total fat 41g Saturated fat 15g Total Carbs 4g Net Carbs 4g Protein 44g Sugar 3g Fiber 0g Sodium: 659mg

GRILL LAMB RECIPES

Lamb Shank

Preparation Time: 10 minutes
Cooking Time: 4 hours
Servings: 6
Ingredients:

- 8-ounce red wine
- 2-ounce whiskey
- 2 tablespoons minced fresh rosemary
- 1 tablespoon minced garlic
- Black pepper
- 6 (1¼-pound) lamb shanks

Directions:

1. In a bowl, add all ingredients except lamb shank and mix till well combined.
2. In a large resealable bag, add marinade and lamb shank.
3. Seal the bag and shake to coat completely.
4. Refrigerate for about 24 hours.
5. Preheat the pallet grill to 225 degrees F.
6. Arrange the leg of lamb in pallet grill and cook for about 4 hours.

Nutrition: Calories: 1507 Cal Fat: 62 g Carbohydrates: 68.7 g Protein:163.3 g Fiber: 6 g

Leg of a Lamb

Preparation Time: 10 minutes

Cooking Time: 2 hours and 30 minutes
Servings: 10
Ingredients:

- 1 (8-ounce) package softened cream cheese
- ¼ cup cooked and crumbled bacon
- 1 seeded and chopped jalapeño pepper
- 1 tablespoon crushed dried rosemary
- 2 teaspoons garlic powder
- 1 teaspoon onion powder
- 1 teaspoon paprika
- 1 teaspoon cayenne pepper
- Salt, to taste
- 1 (4-5-pound) butterflied leg of lamb
- 2-3 tablespoons olive oil

Directions:

1. For filling in a bowl, add all ingredients and mix till well combined.
2. For spice mixture in another small bowl, mix together all ingredients.
3. Place the leg of lamb onto a smooth surface. Sprinkle the inside of leg with some spice mixture.
4. Place filling mixture over the inside surface evenly. Roll the leg of lamb tightly and with a butcher's twine, tie the roll to secure the filling
5. Coat the outer side of roll with olive oil evenly and then sprinkle with spice mixture.
6. Preheat the pallet grill to 225-240 degrees F.
7. Arrange the leg of lamb in pallet grill and cook for about 2-2½ hours. Remove the leg of lamb from pallet grill and transfer onto a cutting board.
8. With a piece of foil, cover leg loosely and transfer onto a cutting board for about 20-25 minutes before slicing.
9. With a sharp knife, cut the leg of lamb in desired sized slices and serve.

Nutrition: Calories: 715 Cal Fat: 38.9 g Carbohydrates: 2.2 g Protein: 84.6 g Fiber: 0.1 g

Lamb Breast

Preparation Time: 10 minutes

Cooking Time: 2 hours and 40 minutes
Servings: 2
Ingredients:

- 1 (2-pound) trimmed bone-in lamb breast
- ½ cup white vinegar
- ¼ cup yellow mustard
- ½ cup BBQ rub

Directions:

1. Preheat the pallet grill to 225 degrees F.
2. Rinse the lamb breast with vinegar evenly.
3. Coat lamb breast with mustard and the, season with BBQ rub evenly.
4. Arrange lamb breast in pallet grill and cook for about 2-2½ hours.
5. Remove the lamb breast from the pallet grill and transfer onto a cutting board for about 10 minutes before slicing.
6. With a sharp knife, cut the lamb breast in desired sized slices and serve.

Nutrition: Calories: 877 Cal Fat: 34.5 g Carbohydrates: 2.2 g Protein: 128.7 g Fiber: 0 g

Smoked Lamb Shoulder Chops

Preparation Time: 4 hours
Cooking Time: 25-30 minutes
Servings: 4
Ingredients:

- 4 lamb shoulder chops
- 4 cups buttermilk
- 1 cup cold water
- ¼ cup kosher salt
- 2 tablespoons olive oil
- 1 tablespoon Texas style rub

Directions:

1. In a large bowl, add buttermilk, water and salt and stir till salt is dissolved.
2. Add chops and coat with mixture evenly.
3. Refrigerate for at least 4 hours. Remove the chops from bowl and rinse under cold water.
4. Coat the chops with olive oil and then sprinkle with rub evenly. Preheat the pallet grill to 240 degrees F.
5. Arrange the chops in pallet grill grate and cook for about 25-30 minute or till desired doneness.
6. Meanwhile preheat the broiler of oven.
7. Cook the chops under broiler till browned.

Nutrition: Calories: 328 Cal Fat: 18.2 g Carbohydrates:11.7 g Protein: 30.1 g Fiber: 0 g

GRILL POULTRY RECIPES

Roasted Tuscan Thighs

Preparation Time: 20 minutes (plus 1-2 hours marinade)
Cooking Time: 40-60 minutes
Servings: 4

Ingredients:

- 8 chicken thighs, with bone, with skin
- 3 extra virgin olive oils with roasted garlic flavor
- 3 cups of Tuscan or Tuscan seasoning per thigh

Directions:

1. Set the wood pellet smoker grill for indirect cooking and use the pellets to preheat to 375 degrees Fahrenheit.
2. Depending on the grill of the wood pellet smoker, roast for 40-60 minutes until the internal temperature of the thick part of the chicken thigh reaches 180 ° F. Place the roasted Tuscan thighs under a loose foil tent for 15 minutes before serving.

Nutrition: Calories 956, Total fat 47g, Saturated fat 13g, Total carbs 1g, Net carbs 1g Protein 124g, Sugars 0g, Fiber 0g, Sodium 1750mg

Smoked Bone In-Turkey Breast

Preparation Time: 20 minutes
Cooking Time: 3-4 hours
Servings: 6-8
Ingredients:

- 1 (8-10 pounds) boned turkey breast
- 6 tablespoons extra virgin olive oil
- 5 Yang original dry lab or poultry seasonings

Directions:

1. Configure a wood pellet smoker grill for indirect cooking and preheat to 225 ° F using hickory or pecan pellets.
2. Smoke the boned turkey breast directly in a V rack or grill at 225 ° F for 2 hours.
3. After 2 hours of hickory smoke, raise the pit temperature to 325 ° F. Roast until the thickest part of the turkey breast reaches an internal temperature of 170 ° F and the juice is clear.
4. Place the hickory smoked turkey breast under a loose foil tent for 20 minutes, then scrape the grain.

Nutrition: Calories 956, Total fat 47g, Saturated fat 13g, Total carbs 1g, Net carbs 1g Protein 124g, Sugars 0g, Fiber 0g, Sodium 1750mg

Teriyaki Smoked Drumstick

Preparation Time: 15 minutes (more marinade overnight)
Cooking Time: 1.5 hours to 2 hours
Servings: 4

Ingredients:

- 3 cup teriyaki marinade and cooking sauce like Yoshida's original gourmet
- Poultry seasoning 3 tsp
- 1 tsp garlic powder
- 10 chicken drumsticks

Directions:

1. Configure a wood pellet smoking grill for indirect cooking.
2. Place the skin on the drumstick and, while the grill is preheating, hang the drumstick on a poultry leg and wing rack to drain the cooking sheet on the counter. If you do not have a poultry leg and feather rack, you can dry the drumstick by tapping it with a paper towel.
3. Preheat wood pellet smoker grill to 180 ° F using hickory or maple pellets.
4. Make marinated chicken leg for 1 hour.
5. After 1 hour, raise the hole temperature to 350 ° F and cook the drumstick for another 30-45 minutes until the thickest part of the stick reaches an internal temperature of 180 ° F.
6. Place the chicken drumstick under the loose foil tent for 15 minutes before serving.

Nutrition: Calories 956, Total fat 47g, Saturated fat 13g, Total carbs 1g, Net carbs 1g Protein 124g, Sugars 0g, Fiber 0g, Sodium 1750mg

Hickory Smoke Patchcock Turkey

Preparation Time: 20 minutes
Cooking Time: 3-4 hours
Servings: 8-10
Ingredients:

- 1 (14 lb.) fresh or thawed frozen young turkey
- ¼ Extra virgin olive oil with cup roasted garlic flavor
- 6 poultry seasonings or original dry lab in January

Directions:

1. Configure a wood pellet smoking grill for indirect cooking and preheat to 225 ° F using hickory pellets.
2. Place the turkey skin down on a non-stick grill mat made of Teflon-coated fiberglass.
3. Suck the turkey at 225 ° F for 2 hours.
4. After 2 hours, raise the pit temperature to 350 ° F.
5. Roast turkey until the thickest part of the chest reaches an internal temperature of 170 ° F and the juice is clear.
6. Place the Hickory smoked roast turkey under a loose foil tent for 20 minutes before engraving.

Nutrition: Calories 956, Total fat 47g, Saturated fat 13g, Total carbs 1g, Net carbs 1g Protein 124g, Sugars 0g, Fiber 0g, Sodium 1750mg

Lemon Cornish Chicken Stuffed with Crab

Preparation Time: 30 minutes (additional 2-3 hours marinade)
Cooking Time: 1 hour 30 minutes
Servings: 2-4

Ingredients:

- 2 Cornish chickens (about 1¾ pound each)
- Half lemon, half
- 4 tbsp western rub or poultry rub
- 2 cups stuffed with crab meat

Directions:

1. Set wood pellet smoker grill for indirect cooking and preheat to 375 ° F with pellets.
2. Place the stuffed animal on the rack in the baking dish. If you do not have a rack that is small enough to fit, you can also place the chicken directly on the baking dish.
3. Roast the chicken at 375 ° F until the inside temperature of the thickest part of the chicken breast reaches 170 ° F, the thigh reaches 180 ° F, and the juice is clear.
4. Test the crab meat stuffing to see if the temperature has reached 165 ° F.
5. Place the roasted chicken under a loose foil tent for 15 minutes before serving.

Nutrition: Calories 956, Total fat 47g, Saturated fat 13g, Total carbs 1g, Net carbs 1g Protein 124g, Sugars 0g, Fiber 0g, Sodium 1750mg

Bacon Cordon Blue

Preparation Time: 30 minutes
Cooking Time: 2 to 2.5 hours
Servings: 6

Ingredients:

- 24 bacon slices
- 3 large boneless, skinless chicken breasts, butterfly
- 3 extra virgin olive oils with roasted garlic flavor
- 3 Yang original dry lab or poultry seasonings
- 12 slice black forest ham
- 12-slice provolone cheese

Directions:

1. Using apple or cherry pellets, configure a wood pellet smoker grill for indirect cooking and preheat (180 ° F to 200 ° F) for smoking.
2. Inhale bacon cordon blue for 1 hour.
3. After smoking for 1 hour, raise the pit temperature to 350 ° F.
4. Bacon cordon blue occurs when the internal temperature reaches 165 ° F and the bacon becomes crispy.
5. Rest for 15 minutes under a loose foil tent before serving.

Nutrition: Calories 956, Total fat 47g, Saturated fat 13g, Total carbs 1g, Net carbs 1g Protein 124g, Sugars 0g, Fiber 0g, Sodium 1750mg

TURKEY, RABBIT AND VEAL

Lightly Spiced Smoked Turkey

Preparation time: 30 minutes
Cooking Time: 6 Hours
Servings: 10
Ingredients:

- Whole Turkey - 1 (10-lbs., 4.5-kgs)
- Vegetable oil – ¼ cup
- The Injection
- Beer – ¾ cup, at room temperature
- Butter – ½ cup, melted
- Garlic – 6 cloves
- Worcestershire sauce – 2 ½ tablespoons
- Creole seasoning – 1 ½ tablespoons
- Hot sauce – 1 ½ tablespoons
- Salt – 1 ½ tablespoons
- Cayenne pepper – ½ teaspoon
- The Rub
- Paprika – 1 ½ teaspoons
- Garlic powder – 1 teaspoon
- Onion powder – 1 teaspoon
- Thyme – ¾ teaspoon
- Oregano – ¼ teaspoon
- Cumin – ¼ teaspoon
- Salt – ½ teaspoon
- Black pepper – 1 teaspoon
- The Fire
- Preheat the smoker an hour prior to smoking.
- Use charcoal and hickory wood chips for smoking.

Directions:

1. Preheat a smoker to 225°F (107°C) with charcoal and hickory wood chips. Wait until the smoker is ready.
2. Place garlic, Worcestershire sauce, Creole seasoning, hot sauce, salt, and cayenne pepper in a blender.
3. Pour beer and melted butter into the blender then blend until smooth.
4. Inject all sides of the turkey—give space about 1-inch. Set aside.
5. After that, make the rub by combining paprika with garlic powder, onion powder, thyme, oregano, cumin, salt, and black pepper. Mix well.
6. Rub the turkey with the spice mixture then lightly brush with vegetable oil.
7. When the smoker is ready, place the seasoned turkey in the smoker.
8. Smoke the turkey for 6 hours or until the internal temperature has reached 160°F (71°C).
9. Remove the turkey from the smoker then let it sit for a few minutes.
10. Carve the smoked turkey then serve.
11. Enjoy!

Nutrition: Carbohydrates: 27 g Protein: 19 g Sodium: 65 mg Cholesterol: 49 mg

BBQ Pulled Turkey Sandwiches

Preparation Time: 30 minutes
Cooking Time: 4 Hours
Servings: 1
Ingredients:

- 6 skin-on turkey thighs
- 6 split and buttered buns
- 1 ½ cups of chicken broth
- 1 cup of BBQ sauce
- Poultry rub

Directions:

1. Season the turkey thighs on both the sides with poultry rub
2. Set the grill to preheat by pushing the temperature to 180 degrees F
3. Arrange the turkey thighs on the grate of the grill and smoke it for 30 minutes
4. Now transfer the thighs to an aluminum foil which is disposable and then pour the brine right around the thighs
5. Cover it with a lid
6. Now increase the grill, temperature to 325 degrees F and roast the thigh till the internal temperature reaches 180 degrees F
7. Remove the foil from the grill but do not turn off the grill
8. Let the turkey thighs cool down a little
9. Now pour the dripping and serve
10. Remove the skin and discard it
11. Pull the meat into shreds and return it to the foil
12. Add 1 more cup of BBQ sauce and some more dripping
13. Now cover the foil with lid and re-heat the turkey on the smoker for half an hour
14. Serve and enjoy

Nutrition: Carbohydrates: 39 g Protein: 29 g Sodium: 15 mg Cholesterol: 19 mg

Tempting Tarragon Turkey Breasts

Preparation Time: 20 Minutes (Marinating Time: Overnight)
Cooking Time: 3½ to 4 hours
Servings: 4 to 5

Ingredients:

For the marinade

- ¾ cup heavy (whipping) cream
- ¼ cup Dijon mustard
- ¼ cup dry white wine
- 2 tablespoons olive oil
- ½ cup chopped scallions, both white and green parts, divided
- 3 tablespoons fresh tarragon, finely chopped
- 6 garlic cloves, coarsely chopped
- 1 teaspoon salt
- 1 teaspoon freshly ground black pepper

For the turkey:

- (6- to 7-pound) bone-in turkey breast
- ¼ cup (½ stick) unsalted butter, melted

Directions:

1. To make the marinade
2. In a large bowl, whisk together the cream, mustard, wine, and olive oil until blended.
3. Stir in ¼ cup of scallions and the tarragon, garlic, salt, and pepper.
4. Rub the marinade all over the turkey breast and under the skin. Cover and refrigerate overnight.
5. To make the turkey
6. Following the manufacturer's specific start-up procedure, preheat the smoker to 250°F, and add apple or mesquite wood.
7. Remove the turkey from the refrigerator and place it directly on the smoker rack. Do not rinse it.
8. Smoke the turkey for 3½ to 4 hours (about 30 minutes per pound), basting it with the butter twice during smoking, until the skin is browned and the internal temperature registers 165°F.
9. Remove the turkey from the heat and let it rest for 10 minutes.
10. Sprinkle with the remaining scallions before serving.

Nutrition: Calories: 165 cal Fat: 14g Carbohydrates: 0.5g Fiber: 0 g Protein: 15.2g

Juicy Beer Can Turkey

Preparation Time: 20 Minutes
Cooking Time: 6 hours
Servings: 6-8

Ingredients:

For the rub

- 4 garlic cloves, minced
- 2 teaspoons dry ground mustard
- 2 teaspoons smoked paprika
- 2 teaspoons salt
- 2 teaspoons freshly ground black pepper
    1 teaspoon ground cumin
- 1 teaspoon ground turmeric
- 1 teaspoon onion powder
- ½ teaspoon sugar

For the turkey

- (10-pound) fresh whole turkey, neck, giblets, and gizzard removed and discarded
- 1 tablespoons olive oil
- 1 large, wide (24-ounce) can of beer, such as Foster's
- 4 dried bay leaves
- 2 teaspoons ground sage
- 2 teaspoons dried thyme
- ¼ cup (½ stick) unsalted butter, melted

Directions:

1. To make the rub
2. Following the manufacturer's specific start-up procedure, preheat the smoker to 250°F, and add cherry, peach, or apricot wood.
3. In a small bowl, stir together the garlic, mustard, paprika, salt, pepper, cumin, turmeric, onion powder, and sugar.
4. To make the turkey Rub the turkey inside and out with the olive oil.
5. Apply the spice rub all over the turkey.
6. Pour out or drink 12 ounces of the beer.
7. Using a can opener, remove the entire top of the beer can.
8. Add the bay leaves, sage, and thyme to the beer.
9. Place the can of beer upright on the smoker grate. Carefully fit the turkey over it until the entire can is inside the cavity and the bird stands by itself. Prop the legs forward to aid in stability. Smoke the turkey for 6 hours, basting with the butter every other hour.
10. Remove the turkey from the heat when the skin is browned and the internal temperature registers 165°F. Remove the beer can very carefully—it will be slippery, and the liquid inside extremely hot. Discard the liquid, and recycle the can.
11. Let the turkey rest for 20 minutes before carving.

Nutrition: Calories: 300 cal Fat: 12g Carbohydrates: 1g Fiber: 0g Protein: 42g

Buttered Thanksgiving Turkey

Preparation Time: 25 minutes
Cooking Time: 5 or 6 hours
Servings: 12 to 14

Ingredients:

- 1 whole turkey (make sure the turkey is not pre-brined)
- 2 batches Garlic Butter Injectable
- 3 tablespoons olive oil
- 1 batch Chicken Rub
- 2 tablespoons butter

Directions:

1. Supply your smoker with Blackstones and follow the manufacturer's specific start-upprocedure. Preheat the grill, with the lid closed, to 180°F.
2. Inject the turkey throughout with the garlic butter injectable. Coat the turkey with olive oil and season it with the rub. Using your hands, work the rub into the meat and skin.
3. Place the turkey directly on the grill grate and smoke for 3 or 4 hours (for an 8- to 12-pound turkey, cook for 3 hours; for a turkey over 12 pounds, cook for 4 hours), basting it with butter every hour.
4. Increase the grill's temperature to 375°F and continue to cook until the turkey's internal temperature reaches 170°F.
5. Remove the turkey from the grill and let it rest for 10 minutes, before carving and serving.

Nutrition: Calories: 97cal Fat: 4 g Protein: 13 g Carbohydrates: 1 g Fiber: 0 g

Jalapeno Injection Turkey

Preparation Time: 15 minutes

Cooking Time: 4 hours and 10 minutes
Servings: 6
Ingredients:

- 15 pounds whole turkey, giblet removed
- ½ of medium red onion, peeled and minced
- 8 jalapeño peppers
- 2 tablespoons minced garlic
- 4 tablespoons garlic powder
- 6 tablespoons Italian seasoning
- 1 cup butter, softened, unsalted
- ¼ cup olive oil
- 1 cup chicken broth

Directions:

1. Open hopper of the smoker, add dry pallets, make sure ash-can is in place, then open the ash damper, power on the smoker and close the ash damper.
2. Set the temperature of the smoker to 200 degrees F, let preheat for 30 minutes or until the green light on the dial blinks that indicate smoker has reached to set temperature.
3. Meanwhile, place a large saucepan over medium-high heat, add oil and butter and when the butter melts, add onion, garlic, and peppers and cook for 3 to 5 minutes or until nicely golden brown.
4. Pour in broth, stir well, let the mixture boil for 5 minutes, then remove pan from the heat and strain the mixture to get just liquid.
5. Inject turkey generously with prepared liquid, then spray the outside of turkey with butter spray and season well with garlic and Italian seasoning.
6. Place turkey on the smoker grill, shut with lid, smoke for 30 minutes, then increase the temperature to 325 degrees F and continue smoking the turkey for 3 hours or until the internal temperature of turkey reach to 165 degrees F.
7. When done, transfer turkey to a cutting board, let rest for 5 minutes, then carve into slices and serve.

Nutrition: Calories: 131 cal Fat: 7 g Protein: 13 g Carbohydrates: 3 g Fiber: 0.7 g

Turkey Meatballs

Preparation Time: 40 minutes
Cooking Time: 40 minutes
Servings: 8
Ingredients:

- 1 1/4 lb. ground turkey
- 1/2 cup breadcrumbs
- 1 egg, beaten
- 1/4 cup milk
- 1 teaspoon onion powder
- 1/4 cup Worcestershire sauce
- Pinch garlic salt
- Salt and pepper to taste
- 1 cup cranberry jam
- 1/2 cup orange marmalade
- 1/2 cup chicken broth

Directions:

1. In a large bowl, mix the ground turkey, breadcrumbs, egg, milk, onion powder, Worcestershire sauce, garlic salt, salt and pepper.
2. Form meatballs from the mixture.
3. Preheat the Blackstone grill to 350 degrees F for 15 minutes while the lid is closed.
4. Add the turkey meatballs to a baking pan.
5. Place the baking pan on the grill.
6. Cook for 20 minutes.
7. In a pan over medium heat, simmer the rest of the ingredients for 10 minutes.
8. Add the grilled meatballs to the pan.
9. Coat with the mixture.
10. Cook for 10 minutes.

Nutrition: Calories: 37 Fats: 1.8 g Cholesterol: 10 mg Carbohydrates: 3.1 g Fiber: 0.6 g Sugar: 1.3g Protein: 2.5 g

SMOKING RECIPES

Blackstone Smoked devil Eggs

Preparation Time: 30 minutes
Cooking Time: 45 minutes
Servings: 8
Ingredients:

- 12 hard-boiled eggs, peeled and sliced in half
- Two jalapeño peppers
- Two slices bacon, cooked crisp and chopped
- 1/2 cup mayonnaise
- 2 tsp. white vinegar
- 2 tsp. mustard
- 1/2 teaspoon chili powder
- 1/2 teaspoon paprika
- Salt to taste
- Pinch paprika
- Chopped chives

Directions:

1. With the roasted peppers, Serving Set the wood pellet grill to 180 ranges F.
2. Preheat for 15 minutes while the lid is closed.
3. Smoke the eggs and peppers for forty-five minutes.
4. Transfer to a plate.
5. Scoop out the egg yolks and location in a bowl.
6. Stir in the rest of the substances.
7. Mash the eggs and blend well.
8. Scoop the egg combination on top of the egg whites.

Nutrition: Energy (calories): 182 kcal Protein: 10.94 g Fat: 14.1 g Carbohydrates: 2.12 g

Cajun Smoked Turkey Recipe

Preparation Time: 10 minutes
Cooking Time: 2-3 hours
Servings: 8

Ingredients

For the injection

- 1 ounce 12- bottle beer, at room temperature
- 1/2 cup butter, melted
- Six large garlic cloves
- 2 tbsp. Worcestershire sauce
- 2 tbsp. creole seasonings
- 1 tbsp. liquid crab boil
- 1 tbsp. Louisiana-style hot sauce
- 1 tbsp. kosher salt
- 1/2 teaspoon cayenne pepper
- 1 pound 12-14 natural turkeys

For the rub

- 1 tsp. paprika
- 1/2 teaspoon garlic powder
- 1/2 teaspoon onion powder
- 1/2 teaspoon dried thyme
- 1/4 teaspoon dried oregano
- 1/4 teaspoon cumin
- 1/4 teaspoon kosher salt
- 1/4 teaspoon freshly ground black pepper
- 1/8 teaspoon cayenne pepper
- 1 tbsp. vegetable oil
- Two fist-sized chunks of applewood or other light smoking wood

Directions

1. To make the injection, place beer, butter, garlic, Worcestershire, Creole seasoning, liquid crab boil, hot sauce, salt, and cayenne pepper in the jar of a blender and puree until completely smooth. Utilizing a meat injection syringe, inject the mixture into the turkey's meat around with each injection spaced about 1-inch apart.
2. To help make the rub, combine paprika, garlic powder, onion powder, thyme, oregano, cumin, salt, black pepper, and cayenne in a little bowl—season turkey inside and out with rub. Fold wings beneath the body, tie the legs together, and brush the turkey lightly with vegetable oil.
3. Turn up smoker or grill to 325degrees F, adding smoking wood chunks when at temperature. When wood is ignited and smoked, place turkey in smoker or grill and smoke until an instantaneous read thermometer registers 165degrees F in the thickest part of the breast, about 2-3 hours.
4. Take away the turkey from the smoker and invite to rest, uncovered, for 20 to 30 minutes. Carve and serve.

Nutrition: Energy (calories): 391 kcal Protein: 11.57 g Fat: 36.76 g Carbohydrates: 2.54 g

CCRyder's Cider-Smoked Ribs Recipe

Preparation Time: 10 minutes
Cooking Time: 2 hours
Servings: 12

Ingredients

- 3 tbsp. white sugar
- 3 tbsp. packed brown sugar
- 2 tbsp. of sea salt
- 1 1/2 tablespoons ground New Mexico Chile powder
- 1 tbsp. garlic powder
- 1 tbsp. onion powder
- 1 tbsp. Hungarian paprika
- 1 tbsp. ground ancho Chile powder
- 1 tbsp. ground black pepper
- 1 1/2 tsp. dried rosemary
- 1 1/2 tsp. dried thyme, or more to taste
- 1 1/2 tsp. ground cumin, or more to taste
- 1 1/2 tsp. ground nutmeg, or more to taste
- 1 1/2 tsp. ground allspice
- 1/2 tsp. cayenne pepper, or more to taste
- Three slabs of baby back pork ribs
- 4 cups apple cider, or as needed
- 2 cups barbeque sauces

Directions

1. Combine the white sugar, brown sugar, sea salt, Chile powder, garlic powder, onion powder, paprika, ancho Chile powder, black pepper, rosemary, thyme, cumin, nutmeg, allspice, and cayenne pepper in a bowl to help make the rib rub.
2. Coat ribs evenly with the rub. Close it with plastic wrap and let marinate in the refrigerator, 8 hours to overnight.
3. Turn to heat the smoker to 300 degrees F (150 degrees C) per manufacturer's instructions. Put the ribs on smoker meat-side up. Cook until browned, about 1 1/2 hour. Then remove from smoker.
4. Pour apple cider into an aluminum roasting pan—position ribs in the pan, sitting on end if needed. Cover with aluminum foil. Go back to the smoker. Just continue smoking ribs until tender, about 2 hours more.
5. Transfer ribs to a grill. Brush barbeque sauce at the top. Grill until darkish, about 10 minutes per side.

Nutrition: Energy (calories): 296 kcal Protein: 4.69 g Fat: 1.55 g Carbohydrates: 68.52 g

Fat Boy's Smoked Baby Backs Recipe

Preparation Time: 10 minutes

Cooking Time: 3 hours and 30 minutes
Servings: 3
Ingredients

- Three racks of baby back pork ribs, outer membrane removed
- 1/4 cup water
- 1/2 cup vinegar
- 1/3 cup Worcestershire sauce
- 1 tsp. olive oil
- 1/2 cup finely chopped onions
- 1 cup ketchup
- 1/4 cup honey
- 3 tbsp. steak sauces (such as a.1)
- 1 tbsp. hot sauces (such as a crystal)
- One clove garlic, chopped
- 1 tsp. ground cayenne pepper

Directions

1. Turn to heat the oven to 200 degrees F (95 degrees C).
2. Place marinated ribs in a shallow baking dish; add water—tent aluminum foil over a baking dish.
3. Bake ribs in the preheated oven until heated through, about 1 1/4 hour.
4. Preheat smoker to 225 degrees F (110 degrees C) according to manufacturer's instructions.
5. Combine vinegar and Worcestershire sauce in a little bowl and pour right into a spray bottle.
6. Transfer ribs to the smoker. Let cook, spraying generously with vinegar mixture every 30 minutes, until tender, about 3 hours.
7. Preheat an outdoor grill for medium-high heat and lightly oil the grate.
8. Heat essential olive oil in a skillet over medium heat. Put an onion; cook and stir until softened, about five minutes. Add ketchup, honey, steak sauce, hot sauce, garlic, and cayenne pepper. Simmer sauce until flavors combine, about 20 minutes.
9. Brush sauce over ribs. Grill until deeply browned, about 15 minutes.

Nutrition: Energy (calories): 336 kcal Protein: 15.36 g Fat: 5.39 g Carbohydrates: 58.84 g

FISH AND SEAFOOD RECIPES

Trager Rockfish

Preparation Time: 10 Minutes
Cooking Time: 20 Minutes
Servings: 6
Ingredients:

- Six rockfish fillets
- One lemon, sliced
- 3/4 tbsp salt
- 2 tbsp fresh dill, chopped
- 1/2 tbsp garlic powder
- 1/2 tbsp onion powder
- 6 tbsp butter

Directions:

1. Preheat your Blackstone to 4000F.
2. Season the fish with salt, dill, garlic, and onion powder on both sides, then place it in a baking dish.
3. Place a pat of butter and a lemon slice on each fillet. Place the baking dish in the Blackstone and close the lid.
4. Cook for 20 minutes or until the fish is no longer translucent and is flaky.
5. Remove from Blackstone and let rest before serving.

Nutrition: Calories 270 Total fat 17g Saturated fat 9g Total carbs 2g Net carbs 2g Protein 28g Sodium 381mg

Blackstone Grilled Lingcod

Preparation Time: 10 Minutes
Cooking Time: 15 Minutes
Servings: 6
Ingredients:

- 2 lb. lingcod fillets
- 1/2 tbsp salt
- 1/2 tbsp white pepper
- 1/4 tbsp cayenne pepper
- Lemon wedges

Directions:

1. Preheat your Blackstone to 3750F.
2. Place the lingcod on a parchment paper or a grill mat
3. Season the fish with salt, pepper, and top with lemon wedges.
4. Cook the fish for 15 minutes or until the internal temperature reaches 1450F.

Nutrition: Calories 245 Total fat 2g Total carbs 2g Protein 52g Sugars 1g Fiber 1g Sodium 442mg

Crab Stuffed Lingcod

Preparation Time: 20 Minutes
Cooking Time: 30 Minutes
Servings: 6
Ingredients:

Lemon cream sauce

- Four garlic cloves
- One shallot
- One leek
- 2 tbsp olive oil
- 1 tbsp salt
- 1/4 tbsp black pepper
- 3 tbsp butter
- 1/4 cup white wine
- 1 cup whipping cream
- 2 tbsp lemon juice
- 1 tbsp lemon zest

Crab mix

- 1 lb. crab meat
- 1/3 cup mayo
- 1/3 cup sour cream
- 1/3 cup lemon cream sauce
- 1/4 green onion, chopped
- 1/4 tbsp black pepper
- 1/2 tbsp old bay seasoning

Fish

- 2 lb. lingcod
- 1 tbsp olive oil
- 1 tbsp salt
- 1 tbsp paprika
- 1 tbsp green onion, chopped
- 1 tbsp Italian parsley

Directions:

Lemon cream sauce

1. Chop garlic, shallot, and leeks, then add to a saucepan with oil, salt, pepper, and butter.
2. Sauté over medium heat until the shallot is translucent.
3. Deglaze with white wine, then add whipping cream. Bring the sauce to boil, reduce heat, and simmer for 3 minutes.
4. Remove from heat and add lemon juice and lemon zest. Transfer the sauce to a blender and blend until smooth.

5. Set aside 1/3 cup for the crab mix

Crab mix

1. Add all the fixings to a mixing bowl and mix thoroughly until well combined.
2. Set aside

Fish

1. Fire up your Blackstone to high heat, then slice the fish into 6-ounce portions.
2. Lay the fish on its side on a cutting board and slice it 3/4 way through the middle leaving a 1/2 inch on each end to have a nice pouch.
3. Rub the oil into the fish, then place them on a baking sheet. Sprinkle with salt.
4. Stuff crab mix into each fish, then sprinkle paprika and place it on the grill.
5. Cook for 15 minutes or more if the fillets are more than 2 inches thick.
6. Remove the fish and transfer to serving platters. Pour the remaining lemon cream sauce on each fish and garnish with onions and parsley.

Nutrition: Calories 476 Total fat 33g Saturated fat 14g Total carbs 6g Net carbs 5g Protein 38g Sugars 3g Fiber 1g Sodium 1032mg

Blackstone Smoked Shrimp

Preparation Time: 10 Minutes
Cooking Time: 10 Minutes
Servings: 6
Ingredients:

- 1 lb. tail-on shrimp, uncooked
- 1/2 tbsp onion powder
- 1/2 tbsp garlic powder
- 1/2 tbsp salt
- 4 tbsp teriyaki sauce
- 2 tbsp green onion, minced
- 4 tbsp sriracha mayo

Directions:

1. Peel the shrimp shells leaving the tail on, then wash well and rise.
2. Drain well and pat dry with a paper towel.
3. Preheat your Blackstone to 4500F.
4. Season the shrimp with onion powder, garlic powder, and salt. Place the shrimp in the Blackstone and cook for 6 minutes on each side.
5. Remove the shrimp from the Blackstone and toss with teriyaki sauce, then garnish withonions and mayo.

Nutrition: Calories 87 Total carbs 2g Net carbs 2g Protein 16g Sodium 1241mg

Grilled Shrimp Kabobs

Preparation Time: 5 Minutes
Cooking Time: 10 Minutes
Servings: 4
Ingredients:

- 1 lb. colossal shrimp, peeled and deveined
- 2 tbsp. oil
- 1/2 tbsp. garlic salt
- 1/2 tbsp. salt
- 1/8 tbsp. pepper
- Six skewers

Directions:

1. Preheat your Blackstone to 3750F.
2. Pat the shrimp dry with a paper towel.
3. In a mixing bowl, mix oil, garlic salt, salt, and pepper
4. Toss the shrimp in the mixture until well coated.
5. Skewer the shrimps and cook in the Blackstone with the lid closed for 4 minutes.
6. Open the lid, flip the skewers, cook for another 4 minutes, or wait until the shrimp is pink and the flesh is opaque.
7. Serve.

Nutrition: Calories 325 Protein 20g Sodium 120mg

Sweet Bacon-Wrapped Shrimp

Preparation Time: 20 Minutes
Cooking Time: 10 Minutes
Servings: 12
Ingredients:

- 1 lb. raw shrimp
- 1/2 tbsp salt
- 1/4 tbsp garlic powder
- 1 lb. bacon, cut into halves

Directions:

1. Preheat your Blackstone to 3500F.
2. Remove the shells and tails from the shrimp, then pat them dry with the paper towels.
3. Sprinkle salt and garlic on the shrimp, then wrap with bacon and secure with a toothpick.
4. Place the shrimps on a baking rack greased with cooking spray.
5. Cook for 10 minutes, flip and cook for another 10 minutes, or until the bacon is crisp enough.
6. Remove from the Blackstone and serve.

Nutrition: Calories 204 Total fat 14g Saturated fat 5g Total carbs 1g Net carbs 1g Protein 18g Sodium 939mg

Blackstone Spot Prawn Skewers

Preparation Time: 10 Minutes
Cooking Time: 10 Minutes
Servings: 6
Ingredients:

- 2 lb. spot prawns
- 2 tbsp oil
- Salt and pepper to taste

Directions:

1. Preheat your Blackstone to 4000F.
2. Skewer your prawns with soaked skewers, then generously sprinkle with oil, salt, and pepper.
3. Place the skewers on the grill, then cook with the lid closed for 5 minutes on each side.
4. Remove the skewers and serve when hot.

Nutrition: Calories 221 Total fat 7g Saturated fat 1g Total carbs 2g Net carbs 2g Protein 34g Sodium 1481mg

Blackstone Bacon-wrapped Scallops

Preparation Time: 15 Minutes
Cooking Time: 20 Minutes
Servings: 8
Ingredients:

- 1 lb. sea scallops
- 1/2 lb. bacon
- Sea salt

Directions:

1. Preheat your Blackstone to 375˚F.
2. Pat dry the scallops with a towel, then wrap them with a piece of bacon and secure with a toothpick.
3. Lay the scallops on the grill with the bacon side down. Close the lid and cook for 5 minutes on each side.
4. Keep the scallops on the bacon side so that you will not get grill marks on the scallops.
5. Serve and enjoy.

Nutrition: Calories 261 Total fat 14g Saturated fat 5g Total carbs 5g Net carbs 5g Protein 28g Sodium 1238mg

Blackstone Lobster Tail

Preparation Time: 10 Minutes
Cooking Time: 15 Minutes
Servings: 2
Ingredients:

- 10 oz lobster tail
- 1/4 tbsp old bay seasoning
- 1/4 tbsp Himalayan salt
- 2 tbsp butter, melted
- 1 tbsp fresh parsley, chopped

Directions:

1. Preheat your Blackstone to 4500F.
2. Slice the tail down the middle, then season it with bay seasoning and salt.
3. Place the tails directly on the grill with the meat side down. Grill for 15 minutes or until the internal temperature reaches 1400F.
4. Remove from the Blackstone and drizzle with butter.
5. Serve when hot garnished with parsley.

Nutrition: Calories 305 Total fat 14g Saturated fat 8g Total carbs 5g Net carbs 5g Protein 38g Sodium 684mg

Roasted Honey Salmon

Preparation Time: 5 Minutes
Cooking Time: 1 Hour
Servings: 4
Ingredients:

- Two cloves garlic, grated
- Two tablespoon ginger, minced
- One teaspoon honey
- One teaspoon sesame oil
- Two tablespoon lemon juice
- One teaspoon chili pastes
- Four salmon fillets
- Two tablespoon soy sauce

Directions:

1. Set your wood pellet grill to smoke while the lid is open.
2. Do this for 5 minutes.
3. Preheat your wood pellet grill to 400 degrees F.
4. Combine all the ingredients except salmon in a sealable plastic bag.
5. Shake to mix the ingredients.
6. Add the salmon.
7. Marinate inside the refrigerator for 30 minutes.
8. Add the salmon to a roasting pan and place it on top of the grill.
9. Close the lid and cook for 3 minutes.
10. Flip the salmon and cook for another 3 minutes.

Nutrition: Calories 119 Total fat 10g Saturated fat 2g Sodium 720mg

Blackened Salmon

Preparation Time: 10 Minutes
Cooking Time: 20 Minutes
Servings: 4
Ingredients:

- 2 lb. salmon, fillet, scaled and deboned
- Two tablespoons olive oil
- Four tablespoons sweet dry rub
- One tablespoon cayenne pepper
- Two cloves garlic, minced

Directions:

1. Turn on your wood pellet grill.
2. Set it to 350 degrees F.
3. Brush the salmon with the olive oil.
4. Sprinkle it with the dry rub, cayenne pepper, and garlic.
5. Grill for 5 minutes per side.

Nutrition: Calories 119 Total fat 10g Saturated fat 2g Sodium 720mg

Grilled Cajun Shrimp

Preparation Time: 5 Minutes
Cooking Time: 25 Minutes
Servings: 8
Ingredients:

Dip

- 1/2 cup mayonnaise
- One teaspoon lemon juice
- 1 cup sour cream
- One clove garlic, grated
- One tablespoon Cajun seasoning
- One tablespoon hickory bacon rub
- One tablespoon hot sauce
- Chopped scallions

Shrimp

- 1/2 lb. shrimp, peeled and deveined
- Two tablespoons olive oil
- 1/2 tablespoon hickory bacon seasoning
- One tablespoon Cajun seasoning

Directions:

1. Turn on your wood pellet grill.
2. Set it to 350 degrees F.
3. Mix the dip ingredients in a bowl.
4. Transfer to a small pan.
5. Cover with foil.
6. Place on top of the grill.
7. Cook for 10 minutes.
8. Coat the shrimp with the olive oil and sprinkle with the seasonings.
9. Grill for 5 minutes per side.
10. Pour the dip on top or serve with the shrimp.

Nutrition: Calories 87 Total carbs 2g Net carbs 2g Protein 16g Sodium 1241mg

VEGETARIAN RECIPES

Blackstone Smoked Mushrooms

Preparation Time: 15 Minutes
Cooking Time: 45 Minutes
Servings: 2
Ingredients:

- 4 cups whole baby portobello, cleaned
- 1 tbsp canola oil
- 1 tbsp onion powder
- 1 tbsp garlic, granulated
- 1 tbsp salt
- 1 tbsp pepper

Directions:

1. Place all the ingredients in a bowl, mix, and combine.
2. Set your Blackstone to 180oF.
3. Place the mushrooms on the grill directly and smoke for about 30 minutes.
4. Increase heat to high and cook the mushroom for another 15 minutes.
5. Serve warm and enjoy!

Nutrition: Calories 118 Total fat 7.6g Total carbs 10.8g Protein 5.4g Sugars 3.7g Fiber 2.5g, Sodium 3500mg Potassium 536mg

Grilled Zucchini Squash Spears

Preparation Time: 5 Minutes
Cooking Time: 10 Minutes
Servings: 4
Ingredients:

- Four zucchinis, medium
- 2 tbsp olive oil
- 1 tbsp sherry vinegar
- Two thyme leaves pulled
- Salt to taste
- Pepper to taste

Directions:

1. Clean zucchini, cut ends off, half each lengthwise, and cut each half into thirds.
2. Combine all the other ingredients in a zip lock bag, medium, then add spears.
3. Toss well and mix to coat the zucchini.
4. Preheat Blackstone to 350oF with the lid closed for 15 minutes.
5. Remove spears from the zip lock bag and place them directly on your grill grate with the cut side down.
6. Cook for about 3-4 minutes until zucchini is tender and grill marks show.
7. Remove them from the grill and enjoy.

Nutrition: Calories 93 Total fat 7.4g Total carbs 7.1g Protein 2.4g Sugars 3.4g Fiber 2.5g, Sodium 3500mg Potassium 536mg

Grilled Asparagus & Honey-Glazed Carrots

Preparation Time: 15 Minutes
Cooking Time: 35 Minutes
Servings: 4
Ingredients:

- One bunch asparagus, woody ends removed
- 2 tbsp olive oil
- 1 lb. peeled carrots
- 2 tbsp honey
- Sea salt to taste
- Lemon zest to taste

Directions:

1. Rinse the vegetables under cold water.
2. Splash the asparagus with oil and generously with a splash of salt.
3. Drizzle carrots generously with honey and splash lightly with salt.
4. Preheat your Blackstone to 350oF with the lid closed for about 15 minutes.
5. Place the carrots first on the grill and cook for about 10-15 minutes.
6. Now place asparagus on the grill and cook both for about 15-20 minutes or until done to your liking.
7. Top with lemon zest and enjoy.

Nutrition: Calories 184 Total fat 7.3g Total carbs 28.6g Protein 6g Sugars 18.5g Fiber 7.6g, Sodium 142mg Potassium 826mg

Blackstone Grilled Vegetables

Preparation Time: 5 Minutes
Cooking Time: 15 Minutes
Servings: 12
Ingredients:

- One veggie tray
- 1/4 cup vegetable oil
- 1-2 tbsp Blackstone veggie seasoning

Directions:

1. Preheat your Blackstone to 375oF.
2. Meanwhile, toss the veggies in oil placed on a sheet pan, large, then splash with the seasoning.
3. Place on the Blackstone and grill for about 10-15 minutes.
4. Remove, serve, and enjoy.

Nutrition: Calories 44 Total fat 5g Total carbs 10.8g Protein 0gSugars 0g Fiber 0g, Sodium 36mg Potassium 116mg

Smoked Acorn Squash

Preparation Time: 10 Minutes
Cooking Time: 2 Hours
Servings: 6
Ingredients:

- Three acorn squash, seeded and halved
- 3 tbsp olive oil
- 1/4 cup butter, unsalted
- 1 tbsp cinnamon, ground
- 1 tbsp chili powder
- 1 tbsp nutmeg, ground
- 1/4 cup brown sugar

Directions:

1. Brush the cut sides of your squash with olive oil, then cover with foil poking holes for smoke and steam to get through.
2. Preheat your Blackstone to 225oF.
3. Place the squash halves on the grill with the cut side down and smoke for about 1½-2 hours. Remove from the Blackstone.
4. Let it sit while you prepare spiced butter. Melt butter in a saucepan, then adds spices and sugar, stirring to combine.
5. Remove the foil from the squash halves.
6. Place 1 tbsp of the butter mixture onto each half.
7. Serve and enjoy!

Nutrition: Calories 149 Total fat 10g Total carbs 14g Protein 2g Sugars 2g Fiber 2g, Sodium 19mg Potassium 101mg

Roasted Green Beans with Bacon

Preparation Time: 15 minutes
Cooking Time: 20 minutes
Servings: 6
Ingredients:

- 1-pound green beans
- 4 strips bacon, cut into small pieces
- 4 tablespoons extra virgin olive oil
- 2 cloves garlic, minced
- 1 teaspoon salt

Directions:

1. Fire the Blackstone Grill to 4000F. Use desired wood pellets when cooking. Keep lid unopened and let it preheat for at most 15 minutes
2. Toss all ingredients on a sheet tray and spread out evenly.
3. Place the tray on the grill grate and roast for 20 minutes.

Nutrition: Calories: 65 Cal Fat: 5.3 g Carbohydrates: 3 g Protein: 1.3 g Fiber: 0 g

Smoked Watermelon

Preparation Time: 15 minutes
Cooking Time: 45-90 minutes
Servings: 5
Ingredients:

- 1 small seedless watermelon
- Balsamic vinegar
- Wooden skewers

Directions:

1. Slice ends of small seedless watermelons
2. Slice the watermelon in 1-inch cubes. Put the cubes in a container and drizzle vinegar on the cubes of watermelon.
3. Preheat the smoker to 225°F. Add wood chips and water to the smoker before starting preheating.
4. Place the cubes on the skewers.
5. Place the skewers on the smoker rack for 50 minutes.
6. Cook
7. Remove the skewers.
8. Serve!

Nutrition: Calories: 20 Cal Fat: 0 g Carbohydrates: 4 g Protein: 1 g Fiber: 0.2 g

Grilled Corn with Honey Butter

Preparation Time: 15 minutes
Cooking Time: 10 minutes
Servings: 6
Ingredients:

- 6 pieces corn, husked
- 2 tablespoons olive oil
- Salt and pepper to taste
- ½ cup butter, room temperature
- ½ cup honey

Directions:

1. Fire the Blackstone Grill to 3500F. Use desired wood pellets when cooking. Keep lid unopened to preheat until 15 minutes
2. Coat corn with oil and add salt and pepper
3. Place the corn on the grill grate and cook for 10 minutes. Make sure to flip the corn halfway through the cooking time for even cooking.
4. Meanwhile, mix the butter and honey on a small bowl. Set aside.
5. Remove corn from grill and coat with honey butter sauce

Nutrition: Calories: 387 Cal Fat: 21.6 g Carbohydrates: 51.2 g Protein: 5 g Fiber: 0 g

Smoked Mushrooms

Preparation Time: 20 minutes
Cooking Time: 2 hours
Servings: 6
Ingredients:

- 6-12 large Portobello mushrooms
- Sea salt
- black pepper
- Extra virgin olive oil
- Herbs de Provence

Directions:

1. Preheat the smoker to 200°F while adding water and wood chips to the smoker bowl and tray, respectively.
2. Wash and dry mushrooms
3. Rub the mushrooms with olive oil, salt and pepper seasoning with herbs in a bowl.
4. Place the mushrooms with the cap side down on the smoker rack. Smoke the mushrooms for 2 hours while adding water and wood chips to the smoker after every 60 minutes.
5. Remove the mushrooms and serve

Nutrition: Calories: 106 Cal Fat: 6 g Carbohydrates: 5 g Protein: 8 g Fiber: 0.9 g

Smoked Cherry Tomatoes

Preparation Time: 20 minutes
Cooking Time: 1 ½ hours
Servings: 8-10
Ingredients:

- 2 pints of tomatoes

Directions:

1. Preheat the electric smoker to 225°F while adding wood chips and water to the smoker.
2. Clean the tomatoes with clean water and dry them off properly.
3. Place the tomatoes on the pan and place the pan in the smoker.
4. Smoke for 90 minutes while adding water and wood chips to the smoker.

Nutrition: Calories: 16 Cal Fat: 0 g Carbohydrates: 3 g Protein: 1 g Fiber: 1 g

BLACKSTONE GRILL COOKBOOK FOR

VEGAN RECIPES

Wood Pellet Cold Smoked Cheese

Preparation Time: 5 minutes
Cooking Time: 2 minutes
Servings: 10
Ingredients:

- Ice
- 1 aluminum pan, full-size and disposable
- 1 aluminum pan, half-size, and disposable
- Toothpicks
- A block of cheese

Directions:

1. Preheat the wood pellet to 165°F with the lid closed for 15 minutes.
2. Place the small pan in the large pan. Fill the surrounding of the small pan with ice.
3. Place the cheese in the small pan on top of toothpicks then place the pan on the grill and close the lid.
4. Smoke cheese for 1 hour, flip the cheese, and smoke for 1 more hour with the lid closed.
5. Remove the cheese from the grill and wrap it in parchment paper. Store in the fridge for 2 3 days for the smoke flavor to mellow.
6. Remove from the fridge and serve. Enjoy.

Nutrition: Calories: 1910 Total Fat: 7g Saturated Fat: 6g Total Carbs: 2g Net Carbs: 2g Protein: 6g Sugar: 1g Fiber: 0g Sodium: 340mg Potassium: 0mg

Wood Pellet Grilled Asparagus and Honey Glazed Carrots

Preparation Time: 15 minutes
Cooking Time: 35 minutes
Servings: 5

Ingredients:

- 1 bunch asparagus, trimmed ends
- 1 lb. carrots, peeled
- 2 tbsp. olive oil
- Sea salt to taste
- 2 tbsp. honey
- Lemon zest

Directions:

1. Sprinkle the asparagus with oil and sea salt. Drizzle the carrots with honey and salt.
2. Preheat the wood pellet to 165°F with the lid closed for 15 minutes.
3. Place the carrots in the wood pellet and cook for 15 minutes. Add asparagus and cook for 20 more minutes or until cooked through.
4. Top the carrots and asparagus with lemon zest. Enjoy.

Nutrition: Calories: 1680 Total Fat: 30g Saturated Fat: 2g Total Carbs: 10g Net Carbs: 10g Protein: 4g Sodium: 514mg

RED MEAT RECIPES

Strip Steak Smoked and Seared

Preparation Time: 10 minutes
Cooking Time: 3 hours 10 minutes
Servings: 2

Ingredients:

- Strip streaks – 2 (At least 1" thick)
- Olive oil – 2 teaspoon
- Kosher salt to taste
- Freshly ground pepper to taste

Directions:

1. Use a teaspoon of olive oil to brush strip steaks on both sides of the season with freshly ground black pepper and salt.
2. Repeat the same process with the other strip steak, then set aside. Place the steaks over the lower rack of the wood pellet grill, and then set the temperature to about 2250F.
3. Smoke the steaks for about an hour or until the internal temperature reaches 1000F. Remove from the grill when ready, and then let them stay warm as you preheat the wood pellet grill to 7000F.
4. Once the grill is heated, switch it to open flame cooking mode, remove the lower racks, and replace it with a direct flame insert. Place back the grates on the grill at the lower position.
5. Sear the steaks as you use tongs to turn them until it develops a nice crust on the outside. Once cooked, transfer the steak strips to a cutting board and rest for about 5 minutes.
6. Add a pinch of kosher salt to the meat, then serve and enjoy.

Nutrition: Energy (calories): 499 kcal Protein: 28.95 g Fat: 41.2 g Carbohydrates: 1.05 g

Smoked Corned Beef Brisket

Preparation Time: 10 minutes
Cooking Time: 4 hours 10 minutes
Servings: 6

Ingredients:

- Corned beef brisket – 4 lb.
- Dijon or horseradish mustard
- Jeff's original rub
- Jeff's original barbecue sauce
- Foil pan or stainless steel

Direction:

1. Put the beef brisket in cold water in the refrigerator and change the water after 30 minutes to remove the extra salt. You can soak it for about 3 hours. You can then coat the entire beef brisket using horseradish mustard.
2. Liberally apply Jeff's original rub to all of the sides. You can pat the rub instead of massaging it into the meat. Set smoker to 2250F with wood pellet smoke, then place corned beef brisket over the smoker grate and let it smoke for about 3 hours or until the temperature of the thickest part reaches 1400F.
3. Make a sauce by mixing Jeff's original barbecue sauce with Dijon, and then create a mustard pad at the pan's bottom and place the meat over the pad with the flat side up.
4. Brush it with more of the mustard sauce, and then cover with foil. Please place it in a smoker and continue cooking for about one hour or until the thickest part's temperature reaches 185oF.
5. Allow the meat rest for about 30 minutes, then slice it and serve.

Nutrition: Energy (calories): 599 kcal Protein: 44.42 g Fat: 45.09 g Carbohydrates: 0.47 g

BAKING RECIPES

Brown Sugared Bacon Cinnamon Rolls

Preparation Time: 5 minutes
Cooking Time: 25 to 35 minutes
Servings 6
Ingredients:
- 12 slices bacon, sliced
- 1/3 cup brown sugar
- 8 cinnamon rolls, store-brought
- 2 ounces (57 g) cream cheese, softened

Directions:

1. When ready to cook, set Blackstone temperature to 350 F (177 C) and preheat, lid closed for 15 minutes.
2. Dredge 8 slices of the bacon in the brown sugar, making sure to cover both sides of the bacon.
3. Place the coated bacon slices along with the other bacon slices on a cooling rack placed on top of a large baking sheet.
4. Place the sheet on the grill and cook for 15 to 20 minutes, or until the fat is rendered, but the bacon is still pliable.
5. Open and unroll the cinnamon rolls. While bacon is still warm, place 1 slice of the brown sugared bacon on top of 1 of the unrolled rolls and roll back up. Repeat with the remaining rolls.
6. Turn Blackstone temperature down to 325 F (163 C). Place the cinnamon rolls in a greased baking dish and cook for 10 to 15 minutes, or until golden. Rotate the pan a half turn halfway through cooking time.
7. Meanwhile, crumble the cooked 4 bacon slices and add into the cream cheese.
8. Spread the cream cheese frosting over the warm cinnamon rolls. Serve warm.

Blackstone Soft Gingerbread Cookie

Preparation Time: 10 minutes
Cooking Time: 10 minutes
Servings 8
Ingredients:

- 1¾ cups all-purpose flour
- 1½ teaspoons ground ginger
- ½ teaspoon ground cinnamon
- ½ teaspoon baking soda
- ¼ teaspoon ground cloves
- ¼ teaspoon kosher salt
- 1/3 cup brown sugar
- ¾ cup butter
- ½ cup plus 4 tablespoons granulated sugar, divided
- ¼ cup molasses
- 1 egg

Directions:

1. When ready to cook, set Blackstone temperature to 325 F (163 C) and preheat, lid closed for 15 minutes.
2. In a medium bowl, stir together the flour, ginger, cinnamon, baking soda, cloves, and salt. Set aside.
3. In the bowl of a stand mixer, cream together the brown sugar, butter and ½ cup of the granulated sugar until light and fluffy. Stir in the molasses and egg and mix on medium speed until combined, scraping down the sides of the bowl.
4. Add the flour mixture to the bowl and mix on low speed until combined. Scrape the sides again and mix for 30 seconds longer.
5. Roll the dough into balls, 1 tablespoon at a time, and then roll the balls in the remaining 4 tablespoons of the sugar.
6. Place the dough balls on a baking sheet lined with parchment paper, leaving a couple inches between each cookie.
7. Place the sheet directly on the grill grate and cook for about 10 minutes, or until lightly browned but still soft in the center.
8. Remove from the grill and let cool on a wire rack. Serve.

Sweet Pull-Apart Rolls

Preparation Time: 5 minutes
Cooking Time: 10 to 12 minutes
Servings 8
Ingredients:
- 1/3 cup vegetable oil
- ¼ cup warm water
- ¼ cup sugar
- 2 tablespoons active dry yeast
- 1 egg
- 3 1/2 cups all-purpose flour, divided
- ½ teaspoon salt
- Cooking spray, as needed

Directions:

1. When ready to cook, set Blackstone temperature to 400 F (204 C) and preheat, lid closed for 15 minutes.
2. Spritz a cast iron pan with cooking spray and set aside.
3. In the bowl of a stand mixer, combine the oil, warm water, sugar, and yeast. Let sit for 5 to 10 minutes, or until frothy and bubbly.
4. With a dough hook, mix in the egg, 2 cups of the flour and salt until combined. Add the remaining flour, ½ cup at a time.
5. Spritz your hands with cooking spray and shape the dough into 12 balls.
6. Arrange the balls in the prepared cast iron pan and let rest for 10 minutes. Place the pan in the grill and bake for about 10 to 12 minutes, or until the tops are lightly golden.
7. Serve immediately.

CHEESE AND BREAD

Blackstone Grill Chicken Flatbread

Preparation Time: 5 minutes
Cooking Time: 30 minutes
Servings: 6

Ingredients

- 6 mini breads
- 1-1/2 cups divided buffalo sauce
- 4 cups cooked and cubed chicken breasts
- For drizzling: mozzarella cheese

Directions:

1. Preheat your Blackstone grill to 375 - 400oF.
2. Place the breads on a surface, flat, then evenly spread 1/2 cup buffalo sauce on all breads.
3. Toss together chicken breasts and 1 cup buffalo sauce then top over all the breads evenly.
4. Top each with mozzarella cheese.
5. Place the breads directly on the grill but over indirect heat. Close the lid.
6. Cook for about 5-7 minutes until slightly toasty edges, cheese is melted and fully hated chicken.
7. Remove and drizzle with ranch or blue cheese.
8. Enjoy!

Nutrition: Calories 346, Total fat 7.6g, Saturated fat 2g, Total Carbs 33.9g, Net Carbs 32.3g, Protein 32.5g, Sugars 0.8g, Fiber 1.6g, Sodium 642mg, Potassium 299mg

Grilled Homemade Croutons

Preparation Time: 10 minutes
Cooking Time: 30 minutes
Servings: 6
Ingredients

- 2 tbsp Mediterranean Blend Seasoning
- 1/4 cup olive oil
- 6 cups cubed bread

Directions:

1. Preheat your Blackstone grill to 250oF.
2. Combine seasoning and oil in a bowl then drizzle the mixture over the bread cubes. Toss to evenly coat.
3. Layer the bread cubes on a cookie sheet, large, and place on the grill.
4. Bake for about 30 minutes. Stir at intervals of 5 minutes for browning evenly.
5. Once dried out and golden brown, remove from the grill.
6. Serve and enjoy!

Nutrition: Calories 188, Total fat 10g, Saturated fat 2g, Total carbs 20g, Net carbs 19g, Protein 4g, Sugars 2g, Fiber 1g, Sodium 1716mg, Potassium 875mg

APPETIZERS AND SIDES

Grilled Broccoli

Preparation Time: 15 minutes
Cooking Time: 10 minutes
Servings: 4 to 6
Ingredients:

- Four bunches of Broccoli
- Four tablespoons Olive oil
- Black pepper and salt to taste
- ½ Lemon, the juice
- ½ Lemon cut into wedges

Directions:

1. Preheat the grill to High with a closed lid.
2. In a bowl, add the broccoli and drizzle with oil. Coat well—season with salt.
3. Grill for 5 minutes and then flip. Cook for 3 minutes more.
4. I have once done transfer on a plate. Squeeze lemon on top and serve with lemon wedges. Enjoy!

Nutrition: Calories: 35g Protein: 2.5g Carbs: 5g Fat: 1g

Smoked Coleslaw

Preparation Time: 15 minutes
Cooking Time: 25 minutes
Servings: 8
Ingredients:

- One shredded Purple Cabbage
- One shredded Green Cabbage
- 2 Scallions, sliced
- 1 cup Carrots, shredded

Dressing

- One tablespoon of Celery Seed
- 1/8 cup of White vinegar
- 1 ½ cups Mayo
- Black pepper and salt to taste

Directions:

1. Preheat the grill to 180F with a closed lid.
2. On a tray, spread the carrots and cabbage. Place the tray on the grate and smoke for about 25 minutes.
3. Transfer to the fridge to cool.
4. In the meantime, make the dressing. In a bowl, combine the ingredients. Mix well.
5. Transfer the veggies to a bowl. Drizzle with the sauce and toss
6. Serve sprinkled with scallions.

Nutrition: Calories: 35g Protein: 1g Carbs: 5g Fat: 5g

The Best Potato Roast

Preparation Time: 15 minutes
Cooking Time: 35 minutes
Servings: 6
Ingredients:

- 4 Potatoes, large (scrubbed)
- 1 ½ cups gravy (beef or chicken)
- Rib seasoning to taste
- 1 ½ cups Cheddar cheese
- Black pepper and salt to taste
- Two tablespoons sliced Scallions

Directions:

1. Preheat the grill to high with a closed lid.
2. Slice each potato into wedges or fries. Transfer into a bowl and drizzle with oil—season with Rib seasoning.
3. Spread the wedges/fries on a baking sheet (rimmed)—roast for about 20 minutes. Turn the wedges/fries and cook for 15 minutes more.
4. In the meantime, in a saucepan, warm the chicken/beef gravy. Cut the cheese into small cubes.
5. It was once done cooking, place the potatoes on a plate or into a bowl. Distribute the cut cheese and pour hot gravy on top.
6. Serve garnished with scallion—season with pepper. Enjoy!

Nutrition: Calories: 220 Protein: 3g Carbs: 38g Fat: 15g

MORE SIDES

Fresh Creamed Corn

Preparation Time: 5 Minutes
Cooking Time: 30 Minutes
Servings: 4

Ingredients:

- 2 - teaspoons unsalted butter
- 2 - cups fresh corn kernels
- 2 - tablespoons minced shallots
- ¾ - cup 1% low-fat milk
- 2 - teaspoons all-purpose flour
- ¼ - teaspoon salt

Directions:

1. Melt butter in a huge nonstick skillet over medium-excessive warmness.
2. Add corn and minced shallots to pan; prepare dinner 1 minute, stirring constantly.
3. Add milk, flour, and salt to pan; bring to a boil.
4. Reduce warmness to low; cover and cook dinner 4 minutes.

Nutrition: Calories 107 Fat 3.4g Protein 4g Carb 18g

Spinach Salad with Avocado and Orange

Preparation Time: 5 Minutes
Cooking Time: 20 Minutes
Servings: 4
Ingredients:

- 1 ½ - tablespoons fresh lime juice
- 4 - teaspoons extra-virgin olive oil
- 1 - tablespoon chopped fresh cilantro
- 1/8 - teaspoon kosher salt
- ½ - cup diced peeled ripe avocado
- ½ - cup fresh orange segments
- 1 - (5-ounce) package baby spinach
- 1/8 - teaspoon freshly ground black pepper

Directions:

1. Combine first 4 substances in a bowl, stirring with a whisk.
2. Combine avocado, orange segments, and spinach in a bowl. Add oil combination; toss. Sprinkle salad with black pepper.

Nutrition: Calories 103 Fat 7.3g Sodium 118mg

Raspberry and Blue Cheese Salad

Preparation Time: 5 Minutes
Cooking Time: 20 Minutes
Servings: 4

Ingredients:

- 1 ½ - tablespoons olive oil
- 1 ½ - teaspoons red wine vinegar
- ¼ - teaspoon Dijon mustard
- 1/8 - teaspoon salt
- 1/8 - teaspoon pepper
- 5 - cups mixed baby greens
- ½ - cup raspberries
- ¼ - cup chopped toasted pecans
- 1 - ounce blue cheese

Directions:

1. Join olive oil, vinegar, Dijon mustard, salt, and pepper.
2. Include blended infant greens; too.
3. Top with raspberries, walnuts, and blue cheddar.

Nutrition: Calories 133 Fat 12.2g Sodium 193mg

SNACKS

Grilled French Dip

Preparation Time: 15 Minutes
Cooking Time: 35 Minutes
Servings: 8 to 12

Ingredients:

- 3 lbs. onions, thinly sliced (yellow)
- 2 tbsp. oil
- 2 tbsp. of Butter
- Salt to taste
- Black pepper to taste
- 1 tsp. Thyme, chopped
- 2 tsp. of Lemon juice
- 1 cup Mayo
- 1 cup of Sour cream

Directions:

1. Preheat the grill to high with closed lid.
2. In a pan combine the oil and butter. Place on the grill to melt. Add 2 tsp. salt and add the onions.
3. Stir well and close the lid of the grill. Cook 30 minutes stirring often.
4. Add the thyme. Cook for an additional 3 minutes. Set aside and add black pepper.
5. Once cooled add lemon juice, mayo, and sour cream. Stir to combine. Taste and add more black pepper and salt if needed.
6. Serve with veggies or chips. Enjoy!

Nutrition: Calories: 60 Protein: 4g Carbs: 5g Fat: 6g

Roasted Cashews

Preparation Time: 15 Minutes
Cooking Time: 12 Minutes
Servings: 6
Ingredients:

- ¼ cup Rosemary, chopped
- 2 ½ tbsp. Butter, melted
- 2 cups Cashews, raw
- ½ tsp. of Cayenne pepper
- 1 tsp. of salt

Directions:

1. Preheat the grill to 350F with closed lid.
2. In a baking dish layer the nuts. Combine the cayenne, salt rosemary, and butter. Add on top. Toss to combine.
3. Grill for 12 minutes.
4. Serve and enjoy!

Nutrition: Calories: 150 Proteins: 5g Carbs: 7g Fat: 15g

DESSERT RECIPE

Pellet Grill Chocolate Chip Cookies

Preparation Time: 20 Minutes
Cooking Time: 45 Minutes
Servings: 12
Ingredients:

- 1 cup salted butter softened
- 1 cup of sugar
- 1 cup light brown sugar
- 2 tsp vanilla extract
- 2 large eggs
- 3 cups all-purpose flour
- 1 tsp baking soda
- 1/2 tsp baking powder
- 1 tsp natural sea salt
- 2 cups semi-sweet chocolate chips or chunks

Directions:

1. Preheat pellet grill to 375°F.
2. Line a large baking sheet with parchment paper and set aside.
3. In a medium bowl, mix flour, baking soda, salt, and baking powder. Once combined, set aside.
4. In stand mixer bowl, combine butter, white sugar, and brown sugar until combined. Beat in eggs and vanilla. Beat until fluffy.
5. Mix in dry ingredients, continue to stir until combined.
6. Add chocolate chips and mix thoroughly.
7. Roll 3 tbsp of dough at a time into balls and place them on your cookie sheet. Evenly space them apart, with about 2-3 inches in between each ball.
8. Place cookie sheet directly on the grill grate and bake for 20-25 minutes until the cookies' outside is slightly browned.
9. Remove from grill and allow to rest for 10 minutes. Serve and enjoy!

Nutrition: Calories: 120 Fat: 4 Cholesterol: 7.8 mg Carbohydrate: 22.8 g Fiber: 0.3 g Sugar: 14.4 g Protein: 1.4 g

Delicious Donuts on a Grill

Preparation Time: 5 Minutes
Cooking Time: 10 Minutes
Servings: 6
Ingredients:

- 1-1/2 cups sugar, powdered
- 1/3 cup whole milk
- 1/2 teaspoon vanilla extract
- 16 ounces of biscuit dough, prepared
- Oil spray, for greasing
- 1cup chocolate sprinkles, for sprinkling

Directions:

1. Take a medium bowl and mix sugar, milk, and vanilla extract.
2. Combine well to create a glaze.
3. Set the glaze aside for further use.
4. Place the dough onto the flat, clean surface.
5. Flat the dough with a rolling pin.
6. Use a ring mold, about an inch, and cut the hole in each round dough's center.
7. Place the dough on a plate and refrigerate for 10 minutes.
8. Open the grill and install the grill grate inside it.
9. Close the hood.
10. Now, select the grill from the menu, and set the temperature to medium.
11. Set the time to 6 minutes.
12. Select start and begin preheating.
13. Remove the dough from the refrigerator and coat it with cooking spray from both sides.
14. When the unit beeps, the grill is preheated; place the adjustable amount of dough on the grill grate.
15. Close the hood, and cook for 3 minutes.
16. After 3 minutes, remove donuts and place the remaining dough inside.
17. Cook for 3 minutes.
18. Once all the donuts are ready, sprinkle chocolate sprinkles on top.
19. Enjoy.

Nutrition: Calories: 400 Total Fat: 11g Cholesterol: 1mg Sodium: 787mg Total Carbohydrate: 71.3g Dietary Fiber 0.9g Total Sugars: 45.3g Protein: 5.7g

Smoked Pumpkin Pie

Preparation Time: 10 Minutes
Cooking Time: 50 Minutes
Servings: 8
Ingredients:

- 1tbsp cinnamon
- 1-1/2 tbsp pumpkin pie spice
- 15oz can pumpkin
- 14oz can sweetened condensed milk
- 2beaten eggs
- 1unbaked pie shell
- Topping: whipped cream

Directions:

1. Preheat your smoker to 325oF.
2. Place a baking sheet, rimmed, on the smoker upside down, or use a cake pan.
3. Combine all your ingredients in a bowl, large, except the pie shell, then pour the mixture into a pie crust.
4. Place the pie on the baking sheet and smoke for about 50-60 minutes until a knife comes out clean when inserted. Make sure the center is set.
5. Remove and cool for about 2 hours or refrigerate overnight.
6. Serve with a whipped cream dollop and enjoy it!

Nutrition: Calories: 292 Total Fat: 11g Total Carbs: 42g Protein: 7g Sugars: 29g Fiber: 5gSodium: 168mg

SAUCES AND RUBS

Herbed Mixed Salt
Preparation Time: 10 minutes
Cooking Time: Nil
Serving: 4
Ingredients
- ½ cup coarse salt
- ¼ cup packed fresh rosemary leaves
- ¼ cup packed fresh lemon thyme
- 1 cup of salt

Directions:
1. Mix the ingredients mentioned above
2. Let it sit and Air Dry for 2 hours
3. Use as needed

Nutrition: Calories: 20 Carbs: 5g Protein: 1g

Classic BBQ Rub

Preparation Time: 10 minutes
Cooking Time: Nil
Serving: 4
Ingredients
- 1 teaspoon salt
- 1/8 teaspoon ground cumin
- ¾ teaspoon ground white pepper
- ¾ teaspoon ground black pepper
- ¾ teaspoon dried thyme
- ¾ teaspoon ground savory
- ¾ teaspoon ground coriander seeds
- 1 teaspoon ground bay leaves
- 1 and ½ teaspoon dried basil
- 2 teaspoons garlic powder

Directions:

1. Mix the ingredients mentioned above to prepare the seasoning and use it as needed.

Nutrition: Calories: 20 Carbs: 5g Protein: 1g

Garlic and Rosemary Meat Rub

Preparation Time: 10 minutes
Cooking Time: Nil
Serving: 4
Ingredients
- 1 tablespoon pepper
- 1 tablespoon salt
- 3 tablespoons fresh rosemary, chopped
- 1 tablespoon dried rosemary
- 8 garlic cloves, diced
- ½ cup olive oil

Directions:

1. Mix the ingredients mentioned above to prepare the seasoning and use it as needed.

NUT AND FRUIT RECIPES

Grilled Pound Cake with Fruit Dressing
Preparation Time: 20 minutes
Cooking Time: 50 minutes
Servings: 12
Ingredients:

- 1 buttermilk pound cake, sliced into 3/4 inch slices
- 1/8 cup butter, melted
- 1.1/2 cup whipped cream
- 1/2 cup blueberries
- 1/2 cup raspberries
- 1/2 cup strawberries, sliced

Directions:

1. Preheat pellet grill to 400degrees F. Turn your smoke setting to high, if applicable.
2. Rub both sides of each pound cake slice with melted butter.
3. Place exactly on the grill grate and cook for 5 minutes per side. Turn 90° halfway through cooking each side of the cake for checkered grill marks.
4. You can cook a couple of minutes longer if you prefer deeper grill marks and smoky flavor.
5. Remove pound cake slices from the grill and allow it to cool on a plate.
6. Top slices with whipped cream, blueberries, raspberries, and sliced strawberries as desired. Serve and enjoy!

Nutrition: Calories: 222.1 Fat: 8.7 g Cholesterol: 64.7 mg Carbohydrate: 33.1 g Fiber: 0.4 g Sugar: 20.6 g Protein: 3.4 g

TRADITIONAL RECIPES

Bacon Wrapped Chicken Breasts

Preparation Time: 0 minute
Cooking Time: 3 hours
Servings: 6
Ingredients:

For Brine:

- ¼ cup brown sugar
- ¼ cup kosher salt
- 4 cups water

For Chicken:

- 6 skinless, boneless chicken breasts
- ¼ cup chicken rub
- 18 bacon slices
- 1½ cups BBQ sauce

Directions:

1. For brine: in a large pitcher, dissolve sugar and salt in water.
2. Place the chicken breasts in brine and refrigerate for about 2 hours, flipping once in the middle way.
3. Preheat the Blackstone grill & Smoker on grill setting to 230 degrees F.
4. Remove chicken breasts from brine and rinse under cold running water.
5. Season chicken breasts with rub generously.
6. Arrange 3 bacon strips of bacon onto a cutting board, against each other.
7. Place 1 chicken breast across the bacon, leaving enough bacon on the left side to wrap it over just a little.
8. Wrap the bacon strips around chicken breast and secure with toothpicks.
9. Repeat with remaining breasts and bacon slices.
10. Arrange the chicken breasts into Blackstone grill and cook for about 2½ hours.
11. Coat the breasts with BBQ sauce and cook for about 30 minutes more.
12. Serve immediately.

Nutrition: Calories 481 Total Fat 12.3 g Saturated Fat 4.2 g Cholesterol 41 mg Sodium 3000 mg Total Carbs 32 g Fiber 0.4g Sugar 22.2 g Protein 55.9 g

SAUCES, RUBS, AND MARINATES

Garlic-Salt Pork Rub
Preparation Time: 5 minutes
Cooking Time: 5 minutes
Servings: 1
Ingredients:

- Eight cloves garlic (minced)
- 1 tbsp. black pepper
- 1 tbsp. paprika
- 1 tbsp. brown sugar
- 1 tbsp. coarse sea salt

Directions:

1. Simply place all ingredients into an airtight jar, stir well to combine then close.
2. Use within six months.

Nutrition: Calories: 20 Carbs: 5g Protein: 1g

RUBS, INJECTABLES, MARINADES, AND MOPS

Dill Seafood Rub

Preparation Time: 10 Minutes
Cooking Time: 0 Minutes
Servings: ¼ Cup
Ingredients:
- 2 tablespoons coarse kosher salt
- 2 tablespoons dried dill weed
- 1 tablespoon garlic powder
- 1½ teaspoons lemon pepper

Directions:

1. In a small airtight container or zip-top bag, combine the salt, dill, garlic powder, and lemon pepper. Close the container and shake to mix. Unused rub will keep in an airtight container for months.

Nutrition: Calories: 20 Carbs: 5g Protein: 1g

Cajun Rub

Preparation Time: 10 Minutes
Cooking Time: 0 Minutes
Servings: ¼ Cup

Ingredients:
- 1 teaspoon freshly ground black pepper
- 1 teaspoon onion powder
- 1 teaspoon course kosher salt
- 1 teaspoon garlic powder
- 1 teaspoon sweet paprika
- ½ teaspoon cayenne pepper
- ½ teaspoon red pepper flakes
- ½ teaspoon dried oregano leaves
- ½ teaspoon dried thyme
- ½ teaspoon smoked paprika

Directions:

1. In a small airtight container or zip-top bag, combine the black pepper, onion powder, salt, garlic powder, sweet paprika, cayenne, red pepper flakes, oregano, thyme, and smoked paprika. Close the container and shake to mix. Unused rub will keep in an airtight container for months.

Nutrition: Calories: 20 Carbs: 5g Protein: 1g

OTHER RECIPES YOU NEVER THOUGHT ABOUT TO GRILL

Decadent Chocolate Cheesecake

Preparation time: 20 minutes
Cooking time 1 hour
Servings: 8

Ingredients

- 1 C. chocolate wafer crumbs
- 2 tbsp. butter, melted
- 4 oz. unsweetened baking chocolate, chopped
- 16 oz. cream cheese, softened
- Three-fourth C. white sugar
- 2 eggs
- 1 tsp. vanilla extract
- One-fourth C. heavy cream
- 2 oz. unsweetened baking chocolate, chopped finely
- One-fourth C. white sugar
- 1 tbsp. unsalted butter

Direction

1. Preheat the grill to 350 degrees F (175 degrees C). Grease a 9-inch springform pan. Sprinkle the chocolate cookie crumbs on the bottom of the pan.
2. Melt the 2oz. of unsweetened baking chocolate and 4 tbsp. of butter till smooth. Stir till.
3. Mix the cream cheese, 1/2 C. of sugar and the 1 tsp. of vanilla. Add eggs and beat till smooth.

4. Add the melted chocolate mixture into the cream cheese mixture. Beat till.
5. Pour the batter into a greased springform pan. Bake for 1 hour. Cool.
6. For the filling: In another bowl, beat the cream cheese, 2 oz. of unsweetened chocolate, 1/4 C. of sugar and 1 tbsp. of butter.
7. Beat until smooth. Add the whipped cream and beat till.
8. Pour the filling onto the cooled crust and refrigerate the cake.

Nutrition: Energy (calories): 625 kcal Protein: 10.5 g Fat: 39.57 g Carbohydrates: 58.12 g Calcium, Ca90 mg Magnesium, Mg102 mg Phosphorus, P234 mg Iron, Fe5.85 mg Potassium, K377 mg

Pork Tenderloin Sandwiches

Preparation Time: 10 MINUTES
Cooking Time: 25 MINUTES
Servings: 6
Ingredients

- 2 (3/4-lb.) pork tenderloins
- 1 teaspoon garlic powder
- 1 teaspoon sea salt
- 1 teaspoon dry mustard
- 1/2 teaspoon coarsely ground pepper
- Olive oil, for brushing
- 6 whole wheat hamburger buns
- 6 tablespoons barbecue sauce

Direction

1. Stir the garlic, salt, pepper, and mustard together in a small mixing bowl.
2. Rub pork tenderloins evenly with olive oil, then seasoning mix.
3. Preheat grill to medium-high heat, and cook 10 to 12 minutes on each side or until a meat thermometer inserted into thickest portion registers 155°F.
4. Slice thin and evenly pile onto hamburger buns.
5. Drizzle each sandwich with barbecue sauce and serve.

Nutrition: Energy (calories): 250 kcal Protein: 39.97 g Fat: 5.54 g Carbohydrates: 7.57 g Calcium, Ca18 mg Magnesium, Mg47 mg Phosphorus, P412 mg Iron, Fe1.92 mg Potassium, K686 mg

Cheesy Ham and Pineapple Sandwich

Preparation Time: 10 minutes
Cooking Time: 2o minutes
Servings: 4
Ingredients:

- 1 (10 ounce) package deli sliced ham
- 4 pineapple rings
- 4 slices swiss cheese
- 4 buns, like potato
- Butter, softened,
- Poppy seeds,

Directions:

1. Cut a large piece of aluminum foil into four squares, large enough to wrap sandwiches in, and place on a flat work surface.
2. On top of each foil piece, stack a bottom bun, 1/4 of the ham, a pineapple ring, and 1 slice of cheese.
3. Place the top bun on top and brush with melted butter; when all sandwiches are built sprinkle poppy seeds on top.
4. Wrap the sandwiches with foil and leave the top slightly loose.
5. Preheat to medium-high and grill for 20 minutes.
6. Let cool slightly, unwrap, and enjoy!

Nutritional Info: Energy (calories): 429 kcal Protein: 10.06 g Fat: 24.82 g Carbohydrates: 42.15 g Calcium, Ca317 mg Fiber1.2 g Magnesium, Mg27 mg Phosphorus, P407 mg Iron, Fe1.23 mg

Garlic Parmesan Grilled Cheese Sandwiches

Preparation Time: 2 minutes
Cooking Time: 7 minutes
Servings: 1
Ingredients:

- 2 slices Italian bread, sliced thin
- 2 slices provolone cheese
- 2 tablespoons butter, softened
- Garlic powder, for dusting
- Dried parsley, for dusting
- Parmesan Cheese, shredded, for dusting

Directions:

1. Spread batter evenly across 2 slices of bread and sprinkle each buttered side with garlic and parsley.
2. Sprinkle a few tablespoons of Parmesan cheese over each buttered side of bread and gently press the cheese into the bread.
3. Preheat the grill to medium heat and place one slice of bread, buttered side down into the skillet.
4. Top with provolone slices and second slice of bread with the butter side up.
5. Cook, 3 minutes and flip to cook 3 minutes on the other side; cook until bread is golden and parmesan cheese is crispy.
6. Serve warm with your favorite sides!

Nutrition: Energy (calories): 507 kcal Protein: 14.94 g Fat: 38.8 g Carbohydrates: 25.72 g Calcium, Ca447 mg Magnesium, Mg29 mg Phosphorus, P641 mg Iron, Fe1.67 m Potassium, K222 mg

Grilled Pizza Cheese

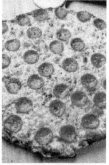

Preparation Time: 10 minutes
Cooking Time: 20 minutes
Servings: 4

Ingredients:

- 8 slices French bread
- 3 tablespoons butter, softened
- 1/2 cup pizza sauce
- 1/4 cup mozzarella cheese
- 1/2 cup pepperoni diced
- Garlic powder, for dusting
- Oregano, for dusting

Directions:

1. Cut bread slices into squares and spread with butter on both sides.
2. Place 1/4 cup pizza sauce, 1 tablespoon mozzarella cheese, and 1 tablespoon diced pepperoni on each square.
3. Sprinkle cheese and pepperoni with garlic powder and oregano as desired.
4. Grill in a pan over medium heat for 5 minutes on each side to melt cheese.
5. Enjoy!

Nutrition: Energy (calories): 210 kcal Protein: 6.56 g Fat: 10.33 g Carbohydrates: 22.75 g Calcium, Ca 145 mg Magnesium, Mg 18 mg Phosphorus, P 104 mg Iron, Fe 1.75 mg

Turkey Pesto Panini

Preparation Time: 5 minutes
Cooking Time: 6 minutes
Servings: 2
Ingredients:

- 1 tablespoon olive oil
- 4 slices French bread
- 1/2 cup pesto sauce
- 4 slices mozzarella cheese
- 2 cups chopped leftover turkey
- 1 Roma tomatoes, thinly sliced
- 1 avocado, halved, seeded, peeled and sliced

Directions:

1. Start smoking your grill to medium-high heat.
2. Brush each slice of bread with olive oil on one side.
3. Place 2 slices olive oil side down on aluminum foil.
4. Spread 2 tablespoons pesto over 1 side of French bread.
5. Top with all the ingredients and repeat with remaining slices of bread.
6. Grill until the bread is golden and the cheese is melted, about 2-3 minutes per side.
7. Serve warm with your favorite salad or soup.

Nutrition: Energy (calories): 886 kcal Protein: 43.57 g Fat: 66.1 g Carbohydrates: 32.8 g Calcium, Ca232 mg Magnesium, Mg102 mg Phosphorus, P456 mg Iron, Fe5.69 mg Potassium, K951 mg

Grilled Veggie Panini

Preparation Time: 12 minutes
Cooking Time: 20 minutes
Servings: 4
Ingredients:

- 8 slices sourdough bread
- 1 small zucchini, cut into strips
- 1 small yellow squash
- 1 red bell pepper
- 1 small red onion
- 3 basil leaves, chopped
- 2 teaspoons olive oil
- Sea salt
- Pepper
- 8 slices provolone cheese
- 2 tablespoons mayonnaise

Directions:

1. Preheat entire grill for medium heat.
2. Toss vegetables, olive oil, basil, salt and pepper in a large mixing bowl.
3. Add to the grill and cook 5 minutes flipping often, until vegetables are softened.
4. Top 4 bread slices with mayonnaise, grilled veggies, cheese, and second slice of bread.
5. Place on the grill and cook for about 3 minutes per side.
6. Remove and serve warm.

Nutrition: Energy (calories): 374 kcal Protein: 16.29 g Fat: 20.62 g Carbohydrates: 31.77 g Calcium, Ca465 mg Magnesium, Mg52 mg Phosphorus, P674 mg Iron, Fe2.21 mg Potassium, K424 mg

Greek Chicken Salad Pita Pockets

Preparation Time: 10 minutes
Cooking Time: 5 minutes
Servings: 6
Ingredients:

- 6 whole wheat pita pockets, halved
- For the sandwich stuffing:
- 1 cup leftover grilled chicken thighs, chopped
- 4 cups shredded romaine lettuce
- 1/4 cup chopped grape tomatoes
- 1/2 cup chopped cucumber
- 1/4 cup black olives, sliced
- 1/3 cup crumbled feta
- 1/4 cup extra-virgin olive oil
- 2 tablespoons red wine vinegar
- 1 lemon, juiced
- 2 cloves garlic, minced
- 1 teaspoon dried oregano
- Sea salt, to taste
- Pepper, to taste

Directions:

1. Whisk together dressing ingredients in a large mixing bowl. Add the sandwich stuffing ingredients to bowl and toss in dressing until well-coated.
2. Fill each pita pocket with Chicken Salad and enjoy!

Nutrition: Energy (calories): 226 kcal Protein: 8.84 g Fat: 11.73 g Carbohydrates: 23.01 g Calcium, Ca 80 mg Magnesium, Mg 37 mg Phosphorus, P 140 mg Iron, Fe 1.73 mg

Mini Portobello Burgers

Preparation Time: 15 minutes
Cooking Time: 15 minutes
Servings: 4
Ingredients:

- 4 portobello mushroom caps
- 4 slices mozzarella cheese
- 4 buns, like brioche
- For the marinade:
- 1/4 cup balsamic vinegar
- 2 tablespoons olive oil
- 1 teaspoon dried basil
- 1 teaspoon dried oregano
- 1 teaspoon garlic powder
- 1/4 teaspoon sea salt
- 1/4 teaspoon black pepper

Directions:

1. Whisk together marinade ingredients in a large mixing bowl. Add mushroom caps and toss to coat.
2. Fire up the grill for medium-high heat.
3. Place mushrooms on the grill; reserve marinade for basting.
4. Grill for 5 to 8 minutes on each side
5. Brush with marinade frequently.
6. Top with mozzarella cheese during the last 2 minutes of grilling.
7. Remove from grill and serve on brioche buns.

Nutrition: Energy (calories): 372 kcal Protein: 3.18 g Fat: 24.08 g Carbohydrates: 35.24 g Calcium, Ca133 mg Magnesium, Mg14 mg Phosphorus, P93 mg Iron, Fe1.35 mg

Layered Beef & Corn Burger

Preparation Time: 20 minutes
Cooking Time: 30 minutes
Servings: 6

Ingredients:

- 1 large egg, lightly beaten
- 1 cup whole kernel corn, cooked
- 1/2 cup bread crumbs
- 2 tablespoons shallots, minced
- 1 teaspoon Worcestershire sauce
- 2 pounds ground beef
- 1 teaspoon salt
- 1/2 teaspoon pepper
- 1/2 teaspoon ground sage

Directions:

1. Combine the egg, corn, bread crumbs, shallots, and Worcestershire sauce in a mixing bowl and set aside.
2. Combine ground beef and seasonings in a separate bowl.
3. Roll beef mixture into 12 thin burger patties.
4. Spoon corn mixture into the center of 6 patties and spread evenly across within an inch of the edge
5. Top each with a second circle of meat and press edges to seal corn mixture in the middle of each burger.
6. Grill into your Blackstone smoker over medium heat, for 12-15 minutes on each side. **Nutrition:** Energy (calories): 433 kcal Protein: 40.16 g Fat: 25.53 g Carbohydrates: 8.62 gCalcium, Ca52 mg Magnesium, Mg40 mg Phosphorus, P312 mg Iron, Fe4.47 mg Potassium,K518 mg

Prosciutto Pesto Hot Dog

Preparation Time: 15 minutes
Cooking Time: 15 minutes
Servings: 4
Ingredients:

- 4 smoked turkey hot dogs
- 4 large hot dog buns or split top hoagies
- 6 ounces fresh mozzarella cheese
- 1/3 cup pesto, divided
- 3 ounces prosciutto, sliced thinly
- 1/4 cup marinate artichoke hearts, chopped
- Olive oil, for drizzling
- Parmesan cheese, shaved for garnish

Direction

1. Heat up the entire grill smoker to medium heat.
2. Add hot dogs, to one side, and reduce that side's heat to low. Grill until cooked through; about 5 to 7 minutes; turning occasionally.
3. Fry the sliced prosciutto until crispy on the other side of the grill; about 3 minutes. Drain on a paper towel lined plate; and set aside.
4. Top the hot dogs with thin slices of the mozzarella cheese, and remove once the cheese is melted.
5. Toast the buns on the grill for 2 minutes and remove.
6. Spread pesto onto the toasted buns.
7. Top with mozzarella covered hot dog.
8. Top with all the remaining ingredients.
9. Serve immediately!

Nutrition: Energy (calories): 267 kcal Protein: 19.76 g Fat: 17.13 g Carbohydrates: 10.22 g Calcium, Ca465 mg Magnesium, Mg41 mg Phosphorus, P376 mg Iron, Fe1.4 mg

Bacon Jalapeno Wraps

Preparation Time: 5 minutes
Cooking Time: 10 minutes
Servings: 4
Ingredients:

- 1 package bacon, uncured and nitrate free
- 6 fresh jalapeno peppers, halved lengthwise and seeded
- 1 (8 ounce) package cream cheese

Directions:

1. Preheat your Blackstone grill smoker for high heat.
2. Fill jalapeno halves with cream cheese.
3. Wrap each with bacon. Secure with a toothpick.
4. Place on the grill, and cook until bacon is crispy, about 5 to 7 minutes per side.
5. Remove to a platter to cool and serve warm.

Nutrition: Energy (calories): 460 kcal Protein: 14.16 g Fat: 43.86 g Carbohydrates: 2.29 g Calcium, Ca 7 mg Magnesium, Mg 17 mg Phosphorus, P 206 mg Iron, Fe 0.52 mg

CONCLUSION

In conclusion, it is a fact that the Blackstone pellet grill has made grilling easier and better for humanity, and Grilling, which is part of the so-called "dietetic" cooking, had been made easier through the Blackstone grill. Giving us that tasty meal, we've been craving for and thus improving the quality of life. This book made you a lot of recipes that you can make at your home with your new Blackstone Pellet grill. The recipes will give so much satisfaction with the tenderness and tasty BBQ.

The Blackstone barbecues are electrical, and a typical 3-position function controls them. A cylindrical device transmits the pellets from the storage to the fire place, like a pellet stove. Blackstone Grill smoker promotes an excellent outcome for your meat and other recipes. This smoker provides a tasty for your foods. To achieve such a real taste, you need the quality of materials and get the exact smoking. It is best if you get the maximum consistency of smoking so that you can have the best result of your meat and other recipes. Moreover, if you add more flavors to your recipes, use the best wood pellet for cooking for your food.

Many people ask me questions on why I chose Blackstone pellet grill, and you might think, well, the answer is clear and true, and yes! It's right before us. Why?

It cooks with a wood fire, giving an excellent quality in taste because nothing is like it: real wood, real smoking, natural aroma. In terms of the cooking process, it has changed a lot. Experts chefs tend to have new experiments with new flavor and ingredients to create a delicious and tasty recipe.

Grilling is one of the most popular cooking processes that grant a perfect taste to your recipes. Grilling is a much healthier method than others because its benefits food, preserves flavor, and nutrients. But from the other side, a Blackstone grill smoker's wood pellet grill allows you to grill your food quickly and with less effort and smoke. The advantage of having a Blackstone grill smoker in your home is the versatility, helps you cook food faster, provides a monitoring scale for the temperature,and it is one of the essential parts of cooking.

It is a versatile barbecue. In fact, it can be grilled, smoked, baked, roasted, and stewed—everything you can imagine cooking with the Blackstone grill smoker. You will find that this Blackstone grill smoker is aflexible tool that has a good service.

As we all could testify that using the pellet grill has been made simple by Blackstone: its intuitive control panel has a power button and a knobthat allows you to adjust the temperature comfortably.

Finally, we need to note that through Grilling, we can always find new flavors in our dishes: with Blackstone pellets, you can smoke your dishes, giving them an ever new and different flavor. Blackstone Grill smoker isthe answer you are looking for your taste buds. Don't waste your time and have your own smoker at home and start cooking your favorite recipes with this book.